CONVERSATIONS WITH MY ELDERS

STONEWALL INN EDITIONS

Michael Denneny, General Editor

Buddies by Ethan Mordden
Joseph and the Old Man by Christopher Davis
Blackbird by Larry Duplechan
Gay Priest by Malcolm Boyd
Privates by Gene Horowitz
Taking Care of Mrs. Carroll by Paul Monette
Conversations with My Elders by Boze Hadleigh
Epidemic of Courage by Lon Nungesser

CONVERSATIONS WITH MY ELDERS

BOZE HADLEIGH

ST. MARTIN'S PRESS
NEW YORK

CONVERSATIONS WITH MY ELDERS
Copyright © 1986 by Boze Hadleigh. All rights reserved. Printed
in the United States of America. No part of this book may be
used or reproduced in any manner whatsoever without written
permission except in the case of brief quotations embodied in
critical articles or reviews. For information, address St. Martin's
Press, 175 Fifth Avenue, New York, N.Y. 10010.

Design by Claire Counihan

Library of Congress Cataloging in Publication Data

Hadleigh, Boze.
    Conversations with my elders.

    1. Homosexuals, Male—United States—Biography.   2. Moving-
picture producers and directors—United States—Biography.   3.
Moving-picture actors and actresses—United States—Biogra-
phy.   I. Title.
HQ75.7.H33   1987   306.7'662'0922   86-26217
ISBN 0-312-00115-0
ISBN 0-312-01404-X (pbk.)

And for my friend E. Z.

2

CONTENTS

Foreword, *by Quentin Crisp*   ix

Acknowledgments   xiii
Introduction   1

Sal Mineo   4
Luchino Visconti   28
Cecil Beaton   56
Rainer Werner Fassbinder   100
George Cukor   132
Rock Hudson   175

Epilogue   208

FOREWORD

 I T has always been my habit to read the main text of any work first and, if I have enjoyed that— and only then—to turn my attention to prefaces, biographies, footnotes and other such peripheral matter.

Publishers evidently do not share my view that this is a common practice. Presumably they think that the purpose of a foreword is, like a second opinion in surgery, to urge doubting patients across unmapped territory with confidence.

This function I now undertake wholeheartedly but with a certain amount of amusement. In his own preamble to these dialogues with the rich and famous, the author states that for a journalist or a biographer to conceal that his subject is homosexual is a political act. Before we ever met I am quite sure that Mr. Hadleigh imagined that I subscribed to this notion. After all, my life has always been an open book—nay, worse than that, it has been a public notice headed by my photograph and the words, "Unwanted, alive or dead," and it is true that, when I was a youth, I thought that what is now known as "coming out" would alter society, but even then I did not expect that people in the public eye would make any declaration concerning their sex lives. That seemed too improbable. Even before we turn the first page of this book, we know why the actors named in it concealed from the world their prevailing sexual inclinations. To suggest that anyone should throw away the world is asking a lot; to demand that they give up Hollywood is expecting the impossible. They did not want to give up their vast wages. They also knew that the deepest fulfillment of their lives would be snatched from them. Even nowadays a man's work is always trivialized by indiscreet revelations. Audiences either shun or eagerly embrace a film involving anyone to whom scandal is attached, not because of the intrinsic merit of his work but because they disapprove of or are intrigued by what they know or think they know about his personal behavior.

When young, I thought that the spreading of the word was a duty that fell to those who, like myself, had nothing to lose. If this attitude now seems odd, it must be remembered that, at the time of which I speak, I was still only English. In Britain, it is the common man who is taken seriously. In that quaint island, directors and producers are assumed to be little better than brothel keepers, and actresses are considered to be prostitutes unless they appear in the works of Mr. Shakespeare. It is only in America that movie stars occupy a position just south of the saints. Hence Mr. Hadleigh's high hopes of them.

Over the past few years he and I have met several times and he now knows that, with the passing of time, I have come to think that both sex and politics are a mistake and that any attempt to establish a connection between the two is the greatest error of all.

Fortunately it is of no importance whatsoever whether or not I or the general reader shares the author's viewpoint. On any level this is a fascinating book.

Its most immediate asset is its gossip value. It allows the uninitiated a glimpse of the private lives of public figures. I always read "keyhole" literature with a furtive eagerness but also with a certain apprehension. I was delighted to find that here questions were asked and answers given without bitchiness or sniggering.

Of more interest to me than discovering new facts about the men whose names form the chapter headings of this book was the manifestation of subtle distinctions between their characters. The interrogation has been conducted so wisely and the replies recorded in such detail that we seem to be hearing the very intonations in which they were given. The words they chose and even the points at which they refused to say more reveal the nationality, the background and the degree of worldliness of each speaker. Signore Visconti and Mr. Cukor were European and this is exhibited in a certain slyness; so was Herr Fassbinder but, because he was younger, he was in a permanent rage. Mr. Beaton, being British, was stuffy and snobbish to the verge of parody. The Americans, on the other hand, were direct and cynical.

Beyond what we learn about all these men is what we discover about Mr. Hadleigh himself because, as Signore Visconti pointed out, these dialogues are not so much interviews as conversations.

The interrogation is by no means self-effacing or neutral. At times it must have been obvious to these men that their opinions and their behavior were being judged and that attempts were being made to bring them to admit regret.

I have known Mr. Hadleigh for some time but we seldom meet, partly because he lives at one edge of the continent and I reside at the other, but also because I live on the eastern coast of middle age, with night already approaching, while he still stands on its western side where dawn has hardly faded. I do not now remember if he originally approached me in order to interview me for some specific magazine, but I was instantly aware of his intense curiosity about life, his courage and his untiring capacity for what I can only call a modern form of evangelism. The elderly know that, if the world changes at all, it will alter for the worse. This is not a prophecy. Decay is a fact of life. However, for those eccentrics who love the human race and wish it well, their hope lies in men like Mr. Hadleigh. It is not by artificially sustaining mere propriety or decorum that, for a little while, the decline of moral values may be deferred, but by an unflagging enthusiasm for the truth, the telling of it even to reluctant ears and by an acceptance of the human condition.

A Jack-the-Giant-Killer excitement is generated by this book. Most of us ordinary mortals would shrink from trying to conduct even the blandest interviews with these distant stars. Hardly any of us would dare to question them with such persistence and such skill as to elicit these intimate and sometimes sad responses.

This book is evidence not only of its author's nerve but also of his charm, which irradiates every page of his work, by which his friends are constantly entertained and which obviously deterred these august personages from ordering him out of their homes.

I hope that my recommendation of this book, in spite of my inability to share its viewpoint entirely, will increase rather than diminish the value of my praise.

—Quentin Crisp

ACKNOWLEDGMENTS

Heartfelt thanks to: my sister Linda Fresia and
Ronald M. Boze and to: Tom Steele, Michael Denneny, and
Athos Demetriou and: Ronnie Blum, Martin Greif,
Armistead Maupin, Patrick Merla, Christopher Nickens,
Charles Ortleb, George Rose, Vito Russo, James Spada, Frank Teti,
Mark Thompson, and Vincent Virga

also: my late grandfather, General Ruben Garcia Lyon, and
Mr. Quentin Crisp.

Portions of the contents have appeared in *The Advocate*,
Christopher Street, *Movie Stars*, *Barbra Quarterly*, and in the book
Streisand Through the Lens.

Introduction

It started in Santa Barbara, a seaside resort ninety-one miles north of L.A. My picturesque hometown had long been a popular location for Hollywood productions. Eventually it even became a TV soap opera. Smogged-out stars came up to film, to talk politics, and to stay.

Our Spanish-style courthouse costarred in "Owen Marshall, Counselor at Law." Our Chamber of Commerce was a background for Rosalind Russell in a scene from her last movie. PBS stationed its cameras in the house of my Santa Barbara High classmate Grant Loud. The Louds had been chosen to become "An American Family." At Santa Barbara City College, I heard Robert Vaughn campaign for McGovern; at SBCC and the University of California at Santa Barbara, Jane Fonda discoursed on McGovern and the Vietnam war. And in and around our elitist suburb of Montecito, a noncommunity of Hollywood refugees took shape. It came to include Janes Fonda and Russell, Robert Mitchum, John Travolta, Lena Horne, Dame Judith Anderson (of "Santa Barbara"), Fess Parker, and the senior Reagans.

I got to meet some of these people, and even talk with them. Almost before I knew what was happening, I was interviewing, acknowledging a journalistic bent inherited from a grandfather who authored forty-two books. Years before earning my master's in journalism, I was free-lancing for a living, doing at first mostly profiles and interviews, which soon led me south.

But although the thrill of meeting Names faded, meeting interesting individuals never palled. As a boy, I'd stared at the photo of my parents at an embassy function, next to Prime Minister

1

Jawaharlal Nehru. *I* never met him, but I did get to interview—for fifteen minutes—his gracious daughter, Prime Minister Indira Gandhi. Yet I might not have, if not for my youth. Initially it put certain interviewees off, but youth did have advantages. It appealed to some people, and made others less wary—thus less reserved. Youth could also elicit the sort of candid answers, or monologues, usually lavished upon a nephew or grandson by one who had *lived*.

After thirty, I began to take stock. Several interviewees had passed away. Halloween 1984 was particularly grim, with the assassination of Mrs. Gandhi. There were the prized personalities I would never meet: Jack Benny, Golda Meir, Vera-Ellen, Tennessee Williams. When George Cukor died in 1983, I thought of the various gay figures I'd interviewed, and a book began to suggest itself.

Then in late 1984, the rumors about Rock Hudson began to proliferate. In mid-1985, the world learned for a fact that he had AIDS. He became the most famous living homosexual, yet over the years I'd managed to publish only one movie magazine interview with him. Editors had said he was "too old" or "washed up," that his private life couldn't be truly told on public pages. Ironically, of all the men in this book, only Hudson might have objected to publication of his franker statements. But then, the greater the fame, the tighter the leash of public affection.

All six men in this collection are gay. They could as easily, if less dramatically, have been British, bilingual, or left-handed. That all were homosexual or bisexual is not a political statement; that virtually all published interviews—and some biographies—deliberately omit a subject's gayness, is.

Other than their sexual orientation, the members of this sextet have little in common. Three were movie directors of different nationalities. Two were actors—or more accurately, *stars*. One was a jack-of-all-arts. Sadly, there is a circumstance which binds three of these men: they died before their time. One was violently murdered. One man destroyed himself after helping destroy his loved ones; it probably wasn't a conscious self-destruction, but Russian roulette.

The most recently deceased subject achieved a monumental but reluctant comeback, via his gradual death. He was destroyed by a new, fatal, and so far inexplicable disease that, outside Africa, primarily attacks gay men. The other three subjects did live to peaceful maturity. But each of these men experienced and accomplished at least a lifetime's worth. This book is dedicated to their enduring spirit.

November 21, 1985
San Mateo, California

Sal Mineo
1939–1976

I MET the Switchblade Kid in 1971, while in a play at Santa Barbara High. Grant Loud was a costar in *The Death and Life of Sneaky Fitch*. The night of the final performance, Sal Mineo was in the audience. He'd come with a friend of Lance Loud, the elder brother whose coming out was a highlight of the series "An American Family." After the set was struck, the blond friend introduced me to Mineo, whom I vividly recalled from *Exodus*. He was shorter than I had imagined, but also better-looking than in that long-ago film. He briefly complimented me on my comedic performance and Western gear.

Later, some two-thirds of us went for beer and pizza, before breaking up into our inevitable cliques. The rest of the cast and crew followed Sal to The Pub, a gay bar popular with Industry types on Saturday nights. A few days later I learned that Sal danced with some of the guys who'd managed to get in, and that unlike many in his profession, he hadn't tried to stand out. After a few drinks and several hot dances—twice with girls—Sal and his friend had left quietly.

At age twenty-one, I finally got to peek inside the forbidden Pub. I was aided and abetted by a former classmate who was related to Sally Struthers. Outside or inside, The Pub was perfectly ordinary: a small bar with a modest dance area, a pool table, and a patio out back. "Big deal," said Dave. "Not even a plaque to let you know that Sal Mineo danced here."

The summer after I graduated from high school, I saw *Rebel Without a Cause* for the first time, on TV. I decided I wanted to interview Sal Mineo. And not because of James Dean; I wasn't a Dean fanatic. At the library, I looked Sal up. I learned that he'd

4

appeared in *The Greatest Story Ever Told* and *Escape from the Planet of the Apes*, two memorable pictures that I didn't remember seeing him in.

A few weeks later, within the space of three days, I saw Mineo in two movies: *Somebody Up There Likes Me*, with Paul Newman as Rocky Graziano, and *Dino*, as a tormented juvenile delinquent. In vain, I tried to contact Lance Loud (we didn't connect until 1975, at a Condé Nast staff party in New York). Next, I tried the blond friend—but he wasn't a student, and locating him was tougher than break-dancing in Venice. At last, I reached Sal Mineo. He took down my number and said he'd probably be able to see me in a few months, before the holidays.

He called in early December 1972. Rather than me going to L.A., he said he'd come up to Santa Barbara. Did I really want to interview him? he asked. Couldn't we just go to a movie or something? Or maybe double-date with some girls he knew? Had I seen the Burt Reynolds centerfold in *Cosmopolitan*? Sal was going to ask Burt to autograph his copy.

"Do you think he will?" I asked.

"Of *course* he will," Sal sniffed.

I suggested that we make a day of it, if he didn't have any other commitments. Sal readily agreed. Like most out-of-towners (and locals over forty), he loved Santa Barbara.

He flew up from L.A. At the time, I didn't consider this unusual. I picked him up in my red Dodge Dart and we went to lunch. Sal made me withhold "all those questions" till later. Then we went to see *Cabaret*. Sal kept nudging me during Michael York's scenes. "What a hunk! *That's* my type." I enjoyed Sal's easygoing company, but fretted that he'd keep postponing our session until he had to leave. So far, I didn't know that much about him, other than his type: blond and supercilious.

In the car, Sal raved about the film. "Liza was friggin' fantastic! Of course—she's a wop. She's gonna win an Oscar. Wait and see. Joel Grey was great—he should win one, too. The director should win one, and so should the movie. The only movie I liked better this year was *The Godfather*." The next year Minnelli, Grey, and Bob Fosse all won Academy Awards for *Cabaret*. Best Picture was *The Godfather*. Sal had never won an Oscar, though he'd been nominated twice.

We quickly reached our destination. It was only a few blocks from the cinema, but Sal hadn't wanted to walk. Even at eighteen, I knew not to ask questions like, "Do you think you'll be recognized?" We entered El Paseo, a downtown tourist trap comprising several shops around a plaza with a small outdoor café. Wearing sunglasses, a white shirt opening on his bronze chest, tight jeans, white socks, and penny loafers, Sal Mineo still looked like the eternal youth.

How do you account for your youthful appearance?

Good genes, I guess. . . . Genes—G-E-N-E-S—by the way!

Does approaching middle age bother you?

As Mae West said, does it bother you? *(Laughs.)*

Or will middle age mean you can finally get away from playing the juvenile?

Good question. I'm only thirty-three—I hope you don't think of that as being middle-aged! It's all in your mind, anyway. Remember when Marilyn Monroe turned thirty-six and she said she looked pretty good for someone her age? That was sad. . . . Maybe you don't remember that.

I certainly remember Marilyn. I'll never forget the morning I found out she was dead. I was in second or third grade, and my family was in L.A. That morning, when we came down into the lobby, the first thing I saw was the headline in the newspaper. It was very sad. It affected me much more than President Kennedy's death.

How come?

Age. To a third-grader, a president, any president, was just some guy in Washington. But Marilyn was the first movie star I knew, and she was so pretty—after she died, I wished I could have been her friend. Probably everybody's felt that way. . . . How did her death affect you, Sal?

I cried. She was a nice kid, a good kid. I met her, of course. But . . . we never worked together. How about you—did *you* cry?

No. Not when she died. Afterward, when we were visiting some friends of my parents, and these people were making very

disparaging remarks about her. I cried then. I couldn't understand
why they'd want to do that.

Everyone forgets—fortunately, I guess—that Marilyn was not
only a sex symbol, she was real controversial. Especially when she
started out. I remember, because movie people were split fifty-fifty
for and against her.

The double standard: since she was a sexy woman, she was
looked on as some kind of prostitute, by some.

And then as she grew more celebrated or whatever, some of the
people who'd liked her turned on her. Because she'd be notoriously
late on the set—man, I could never get away with that. But I never
thought less of her for it. . . . Did you ever cry after Kennedy died?

Did you?

Yeah. But I cry easy. Comes from being a wop.

Well, as I said, I came to appreciate President Kennedy after
reading about him. At the time, when I saw the coverage on TV,
what amazed and kind of pleased me was how all those grown
people were crying, even men. I didn't believe most grown-ups
had the tenderness to be able to cry.

Nice discovery. . . . Well, like you say, as I get older, the range
of roles for me will hopefully open up. But I'm sick of waiting, and
they still think of me like I only did a couple of roles, and the rest
of my career was all reruns.

Still the Switchblade Kid, huh?

(Smiles.) That's right! Still the best pal to the lead. (Shakes head.)
Hollywood don't flex its muscle-brain.

How do you mean?

What you start out as is pretty much how you wind up. I mean,
you get typed in the first thing that clicks, then they don't give
you no more fuckin' chances.

It's harder for those who begin very young, isn't it?

Everyone knows that. Almost no kid star ever becomes an adult
star—the ones that do are all girls.

Your first film was?

Six Bridges to Cross. God, don't remind me. Jeez . . . They should have titled it *Six Bridges to Burn.* But I was lucky, 'cause then came *Rebel.*

So much has been said and written about that film.

You're telling me. . . . Why don't you ask me about that later? I get these interviewers who just want to ask about Dean and *Rebel*, and they go on and on, like they were writing a book!

Do you ever think that, if you hadn't been in *Rebel*, you might have become a bigger star?

You mean I might've had the *lead.* When I started in films I was fifteen, sixteen, and I had this baby face that made me look like a wheat-flour dumpling or something. And the name didn't exactly help.

That's true. . . . Come to think of it, you're almost the only Italian-American actor who was allowed to keep his surname. Did you put up a big fight to retain it?

Damn right, man. I'm proud of being a wop.

First time I heard "wop," I thought it was a kind of little fish —like a pollywog.

Pollywop's an Italian parrot. . . . Yeah, I was unique. They made all the guys change names and half of them had to have nose jobs, like Dean Martin, alias Dino Crocetti. And the girls: Anne Bancroft's real name was Italiano—and Paula Prentiss' was Ragusa, I think.

What did they think they were accomplishing by doing that, I wonder? Particularly since most of the studio heads weren't WASPs.

Standardization.

Easier to control people when you can keep them fitting into molds, I suppose.

Hell, not just that, they didn't want the world to know there was an Italian heritage. *Or* that you could look all kinds of ways and be Italian. We ain't all olive-skinned. Look at Connie Stevens or what's-her-name . . . Bernadette Peters.

And look at Virna Lisi, fresh from the old country.

You are making me horny. . . .

Who are those two girls you mentioned, for a double date?

(Laughs.) Are you kidding? I got a girl in every port—and a couple of guys in every port, too.

Do you think rumors about being bi have hurt you in your career?

Maybe . . . Nah, I doubt it. Everyone's got those rumors following him around, whether it's true or not. *Every*one's supposed to be bi, starting way back with Gary Cooper and on through Brando and Clift and Dean and Newman and . . . you want me to stop?

Did you resent the rumors?

Well, no. Because what's wrong with being bi? Maybe most people are, deep down.

Shirley MacLaine has publicly said that.

I think she's right—got a good noodle, Shirl does. But anyhow, the rumor about me, from what I hear, was usually that I'm gay. Where, like, with Monty Clift or Brando, the rumor was that they're bi. [Brando later publicly admitted to bisexuality.]

There was also a rumor that you once hustled. . . .

Hustled? *Me?* No. I never charged no one in my life—and I could have, too. But I tell you this: some of my relatives, over in Sicily, are *ragazzi di vita.*

"Boys of life?"

Yeah—means hustlers. *(Shrugs.)* A lot more of that goes on than people think, especially in poor places.

What about Hollywood's male casting couch?

What about it? There's always been a casting couch—gay, bi, straight, everything.

Even women behind the casting couch now, I hear.

Yeah, but not much. They gotta keep more careful about their reps than men do. Anyway, if you want to know if I've been on the couch, unh-unh.

Careers can't be built on couches, right?

You got it. I mean, a chick or a guy can get some tiny part or get put in front of a crowd, *maybe*. But that's it. And it's blackmail—you gotta keep playing the guy's game. It wouldn't be worth it. And it would mean you can't get by on your talent.

Have you felt being stereotyped limited your talent?

No one ever said movies are for developing your range. Hardly anyone gets that opportunity. Which is why I think the stage is so good. It's less bread, but you can play different types, and you can initiate your own projects.

Have you given up on movies?

I've never given up completely. It's hard to let go. Maybe if I had, if I'd gone and become some top-notch stage actor, then they'd have rediscovered me. That can happen.

Escape from the Planet of the Apes **was a hit. Will you do more of those?**

Eh, sequels . . . I'll bet you didn't exactly recognize me in it. I doubt I'll do another; it's pretty thankless. Frankly, I did it for the bread.

You didn't become a millionaire with all those movies?

Not many did. It's just that you keep hearing about the ones who did. And now they earn obscene kinds of bread, and there's a bigger difference now between what a big star earns and a . . . lesser star. Who says it's a democratic business?

You've also spent quite a bit on your family?

You read that? (*Smiles.*) Where'd you read that?

Years back, I guess. About how you bought your mom a home and provided for your sister and brother—

Brothers. Yeah, well, we wops stick together. Least I could do.

Now, you know, what I remember you best from was *Exodus*.

My parents took us to see it when it came out, and it made a *big* impression on me.

What part did you like best?

Well, not a *part,* or even all the fine actors in it, but the story, the drama about reestablishing Israel, and what they had to go through to do it. The shocking part, to me, was how unfair the British were—up till then, I'd always thought they were *more* civilized.

It's a terrific story, and Otto Preminger made it more than just a movie, but you know what shocked a lot of people then? *My* part: where Dov Landau confesses that the Nazis used him "like a woman." The word *homosexual* had hardly been mentioned in anything then, and when I said that . . . the speech, you could *hear* the shock.

It must've shocked the Academy into nominating you for an Oscar.

It sure helped. *Sympathy.* For the character, who died in the end—pardon the pun. He *had* to die, even though he was straight and in love with this blond girl, because he was, shall we say, tainted. In the censors' eyes, anyway.

Hollywood morality . . . The funny thing is, when I saw it at the cinema, the rape part went right past me. Kids don't *get* that. Later, when I saw it on TV, years ago, already, it was like hearing that part of the movie for the first time.

Was the first time you heard it. Yeah, Preminger had a lot of guts. He was real anti-censor, 'cause he was so pro-liberty, and years before *Exodus* he was testing the censors with his subject matter. He was the first one to prove you didn't need the god-damned Seal [the Production Code Seal of Approval] for commercial success. He helped end movie censorship.

A remarkable man. Who won the Best Supporting Actor Oscar that year?

Mr. Peter Ustinov. *Spartacus*—guys who didn't like Kirk Douglas called it *Sparagus.* But Peter's okay—a good actor. *He* won *two* Oscars. I guess that proves he's good.

Who won when you were nominated for *Rebel*? Then we'll get off this depressing subject.

Ta-da: Jack Lemmon, in *Mister Roberts*. I knew he'd win.

Coincidentally—or not—your character, Plato, was killed off in *Rebel*, too.

Makes sense: he was, in a way, the first gay teenager in films. You watch it now, you *know* he had the hots for James Dean. You watch it now, and everyone knows about Jimmy, so it's like *he* had the hots for Natalie [Wood] and me. Ergo, I had to be bumped off, out of the way.

Straight critics and audiences would mostly see that Plato was looking for a father figure, since he comes from a broken home.

The brokenest! So what's the point?

I think people tend to see what they want to see. Plato's feelings may be a mixture of seeking the missing father and idolizing or adoring Jim, but straights will see only the one aspect and gays will see only the other. What do you think?

Does that mean only bisexuals see both aspects?

Could be. . . .

I do think *Rebel*'s one of those superflicks that are all things to all people. It has so many levels.

So in a sense, your career began at the top . . .

And I've been working my way down ever since.

I didn't mean that. But people who peak early—like you, with your Oscar nominations within five or six years of each other— often find it difficult to live up to the early promise, right?

Don't I know. . . . No, you're absolutely right. You only get a *Rebel* or an *Exodus* once in a few years, and if you can work up to that, people see you as developing. If it starts out that way, they see you as, well, regressing. Those are maybe my most famous flicks, and I played fucked-up teens in them, so guess what they kept offering me?

I found *Dino* very touching—the best thing I've ever seen on juvenile delinquency and the vicious circle of reform schools.

It was pretty decent. But you know what I liked? *The Gene Krupa Story.* I loved those drums, man!

I haven't seen that. I almost saw one of yours called *Tonka.* Didn't have any idea what it was about, but I used to play with Tonka trucks when I was a kid, so . . .

Why didn't you see it?

I went out on a date that night.

So tell me.

I had a date with this girl on Saturday night, but she wanted to change it to Friday, because of a family visit. But I'm sure I'll catch up with *Tonka* someday.

Eh, don't bother. If you've got a heavy date, go with it, man. Or her, or him, or whatever.

Do *you* think bisexuality is the true norm?

You mean do I think everyone's bi? Yeah . . . if they'd be honest about it, or try it. How about you?

I don't think one can generalize about people that way.

How about you personally?

I've been attracted to both. . . . Now, back to your career. Did you think of yourself as a sex symbol?

An SS? *(Laughs.)* Not after I made *Exodus.* You know, Otto *sounds* like a Nazi, and he's a tough buzzard, but he's got a great heart. Nice man. . . . What were we talking about? Oh, yeah. *Did* or *do* I consider myself sexy?

Do you consider yourself a sex symbol?

Only when I'm alone and lonely . . . if you know what I mean.

Who doesn't?

Oh, I know a few devout Sicilians who don't. . . .

Priests?

Are you kidding? *Nuns.* Priests do it right and left—there's more gay priests than you can figure. Why do you think the Church is so down on priests?

Appearances?

Yeah, that and the clothes they wear. Anyway, I don't want to offend anybody here. . .

Well, speaking of headgear, anyway, you did *Escape from Zahrain* with Yul Brynner. I think he kept that hood on his head through the whole movie! What's the story?

That flick was not made in the shade, man. Desert heat, and then some. I don't think Yul wanted to bother shaving two, three times a day.

You're right—he had a beard, too.

Mostly I think he wanted to look exotic.

I don't think he could help that. . . .

And it was a scene-stealing thing: everyone kept wondering if he'd ever remove the friggin' hood.

What was it like working with Paul Newman in *Somebody Up There Likes Me?*

You didn't even comment that I did two flicks with *Escape* in the title. *(Smiles.)* Paul was pretty new then. Like me. Only, he was taller and he had blue eyes, and being half-Gentile, he could get into leading-man parts just like that. *(Snaps fingers.)*

He certainly had the required look.

And then some. And don't think he didn't know it. Well, the truth is, we didn't get along that great.

That sort of parallels the fact that Rock Hudson and James Dean didn't get along on *Giant.* Older man/younger man rivalry?

Maybe. But Paul—I gotta be fair to the man—he had a heavy part, with makeup and cauliflower ears and all, so he had lots to worry about. Plus he was runnin' sorta scared, with one big bomb behind him. We were all impressed out of our wits—I came from the stage, and Hollywood was *it*. I'd have done anything they wanted.

Was Newman approachable? I've heard he has a considerable ego.

We all have that. But yeah, he was on kind of a star trip. He could afford to be. Leading men can survive a few flops. Me, if I'd had a few flops back then, I'd have been demoted to bit parts or stuck in some crowd scene.

I once came across a color picture in a movie book of you and Barbara Eden and other actors and actresses, all in swimsuits, posing for a cheesecake or beefcake shot. Your arms were all linked, and—

Jesus, that was long ago! I haven't seen that picture in, God, I don't know how long. We were all on this artificial beach set. I have to admit, I looked pretty cool, even back then.

You're one of those people who look better, the older they get.

Thanks. Yeah, so far. But did you get a load of Eden's hips? Widesville, man.

Her hair was darker, too, and she wasn't at all as attractive as she is now. What happened?

They go to work on the dames the moment they set foot in the studio gate. They starve them, they set these fag beauty experts on them, and they tell them to get gorgeous or else no dice.

Anything comparable for the men?

Lose the weight—but not too much. I've never had any real weight problem. Wait till your mid-twenties, then *you'll* know. Something happens around twenty-five, and you can never eat the same way again. Or if you do, the weight starts creeping up on you, faster and faster—according to my friends.

They must have shaved your chest in that beach shot.

Hair is—*was*—"vulgah ."

They didn't try to change your New York accent?

They tried to change everything except my fuckin' gender! But they finally figured out that maybe what I had worked. And it did, for the kind of things I did at first, and kept on doing.

Some more titles of your movies: *The Longest Day, Crime in the Streets, The Young Don't Cry* . . . **Rather grim titles. Anything you want to say about any of them?**

Just watch them, if you like. They're self-explained. Most of them are so-so.

Krakatoa, East of Java. **Probably a disaster film ahead of its time, huh?**

Nobody remembered Krakatoa—sounded like a voodoo flick to most people.

I did see *The Greatest Story Ever Told.*

You Catholic, too?

My mother is. Why?

It could've broken even if all the Catholics and their families had seen it.

I did my part—I saw it twice.

Once for the plot and once for the scenery? *(Laughs.)* I played Uriah; it was an all-star thing. Everyone was in it. And it offended just about everyone—either that, or they just didn't give a damn.

It was a 1965 film. I guess Biblical pictures were completely out of favor by then. Prophets became losses.

Very good! *(Both laugh.)*

It's not mine—someone told me that one. But George Stevens, of *Giant,* **directed** *Story.*

What was he like to work with? Well, I didn't exactly have a starring role. That was Max von Sydow, who's a nice guy. A lot nicer than the last guy who'd played Jesus. . . .

Jeffrey Hunter, in *King of Kings.*

Yeah, young blue-eyes. Gorgeous. A creep.

He was bisexual, wasn't he?

Yeah. Anyway, Stevens was good—I mean, a good director. But a tough old buzzard. The best directors are usually tough nuts to crack, but the result's usually worth it, after.

Pat Boone was in *Story*, and so was Charlton Heston and . . .

I just said: *every*one was in it. Heston, he has an ego the size of Texas and a talent the size of South Dakota.

Why not North Dakota?

We won't go into that. Anyhow, Boone, well, everyone knows what a bigot he's turned out to be. . . . Who else was in that? Let's see: Victor Buono—I forget what he played, but he's cool; real fat, so he looks twice his age. Angela Lansbury—real nice lady, nothing like her bitchy [movie] image. Not that I worked with hardly any of these guys, but I've at least met them all. Of course, Roddy McDowall was in it—you know Roddy?

I just know of him.

Everyone knows *of* him . . . *(Smiles.)* Carroll Baker was in it— the obligatory sex symbol, right? She played, uh, Veronica. . . . They even got Sidney Poitier into it. I ought to see it again some time, for laughs. Everybody's in it; it would probably become a cult movie, if it weren't religious.

Are you religious?

Privately, yeah. I'm sure no stickler for all those Catholic rules, anyway.

Briefly getting back to *Rebel Without a Cause* . . .

Oh, no . . . *(Groans, then laughs.)* In my case, *Rebel Without a Pause*. Well, what?

Do you agree with the statement that the characters played by you and Dean and Natalie Wood were forming your own nuclear family in *Rebel*, since they all came from broken homes?

That's a good concept, but I don't know that it was what [Nicholas] Ray and everyone intended.

Because Dean and Wood were about the same age, and you were younger, looking up to him . . .

One thing, though: if it's some nuclear unit or whatever, the son gets killed off.

Homophobia, I suppose. You'd prove a rival to Natalie for Jimmy. And the idea is that they live happily ever after, meaning that they'll reproduce and have their own kids.

Yeah, so how's that make it a nuclear family unit?

It could as easily be seen as a triangle. But when it was made, there were no homosexual characters, ever.

If there had been, I might've been called a *name!*

That's what eventually happened; it went from invisibility on the screen to name-calling and vituperation. If Plato had been an actually gay role, would you have accepted it?

Probably. . . . Listen, I'd have done anything to get into movies and stay there. And if it's a big-budget flick with top names, you take anything in it—unless you're a big star.

Don't you think a lot of gay actors totally shy away from gay roles?

You know they do. Rock Hudson, X, Y, Z . . . Not me—not anymore, if I ever did. Dov was *not* a gay role. . . .

Even though he was sacrificed to homophobia. . . . What do you think of recent gay films like *The Boys in the Band* or *Myra Breckinridge*?

Myra ain't gay. That was transsexual stuff, and it was mostly Raquel Welch.

And Myron—Rex Reed—was more like her boyfriend than her prior self.

Right. But Mae West was a hoot in it. I got friends who go up and see her—gay guys, jocks.

Gay jocks?

Yeah. They adore her, so she gets the reaction she wants out of them. Most straight guys would gross out if she made a move on them. But *Boys in the Band* was fun. It was kind of negative, because it was one of the first movies like that—or plays. I think we'll see more and more of the gay stuff up on the screen, because people are curious, and gays go to see anything about themselves—especially if it's funny or sexy.

You, of course, produced another stage version of *Fortune and Men's Eyes,* **and it was a hit.**

Like I said, sexy—we put in nudity and everything. I mean, that's what they want. You don't do a thing about men behind bars and hold back on the sex and the raunch. They know what they're expecting to see—the audiences, I mean.

You had nothing to do with the movie version. What did you think of the movie?

Flop time. Unh-unh. Nothin' like my play—my version. Less integrity.

Were you approached to costar in it?

Dino Grows Up—the Hard Way! (Both laugh.) Well, they knew I did the play, and I'd want some input. The producers of the flick-flop flop-flick knew exactly what they wanted. It sure wasn't what audiences wanted.

By doing *FaME,* **you were virtually announcing your sexuality to the public. Did you worry about that?**

It wasn't like producing or directing a gay movie—it got a lot less publicity. The public hardly ever knows anything about that; if they see me kiss a girl in a movie, that's what they remember, and that's what they assume.

But more importantly, you were letting Hollywood know that you didn't care who knew. Wouldn't that rob you of future movie roles?

Sure. Once I did *FaME,* I probably lost half my future chances. But that'll change—it's already changing. I think it's only going to change in a big way—in the future, I mean—if gay actors and stars and directors *come out.* That'll show the guys in charge that we're here, and we're gonna stick around and not keep playing bury-the-queer-in-the-fairy-tale. You know what I'm saying?

Yes, I do. Do you like directing as well as acting?

I like not being bossed around all the time. I'll never be Nick Ray or George Stevens, but I'd like to direct some good pictures. It doesn't matter if I'm in them. *FaME* was a great experience, and I liked working with actors instead of just competing with them. Yeah, I want to do lots more of that. Even if I never act again, though I'd hate not having a choice.

Having a choice—isn't that what your being involved with gay themes is about? Or, for that matter, being bisexual?

I think so. I don't like having to just do straight parts, or gay parts, and I don't like to be told I can only love a woman—or a guy.

Why do you think so many gay men are turned off by bisexual men?

Listen, they ain't turned off by them *sexually*. Maybe politically. Because half the gays in Hollywood pretend they're bi. And I guess so far that's a matter of survival. Some don't even have the guts to say they're bi.

By the same token, some straight men, mostly younger, trendy ones, like to *say* they're bisexual.

That's cool. Even if it ain't true, some of them try it, once or twice, and that's healthy. It lets them find out if they really got no taste for men, or if they're really bi or gay, but they've been fooling themselves—like the "straight" guy in *Boys in the Band.*

Do you believe in trying everything once?

You mean drugs, don't you? *(Shrugs.)* Why not? Once, anyway. I'm not into heavy drugs. You can't be, and still work. And I *like* working. It lets you show what you're made of, and it's a challenge. I mean, fuckin' Hollywood has its faults, but I love being part of the entertainment industry. No way I'd want to try something else—I *know*, from my relatives. Hardly any of them are happy at what they're doing.

Somebody in L.A. told me you'd wanted to be in *Midnight Cowboy?*

I was, once, interested in buying the rights. Did you ever read that novel? James Leo Herlihy—nice guy. The book's fuckin' fantastic, man. Even better than the movie. Anyway, I'd wanted to play Ratso.

Why not the Jon Voight part?

Do you see blond hair on this head, huh? It's a WASP part, and Ratso's a wop or a Jew. That ain't just my opinion, that's how Hollywood works.

What was your childhood like in New York?

My childhood in New York was one long *Bronx* cheer. Okay?

You're probably a lot more interesting now. . . . Was Paul New-man any nicer in *Exodus*?

Everyone has a Paul Newman thing, man. *(Shakes head.)* He's a great-looking ice cube. Leave it at that.

You played Broadway, didn't you? A prince in *The King and I*?

You're from the East, you do "theatah," eventually you hit Broadway. It ain't as exciting as it sounds.

Maybe *this* isn't as exciting as it sounds, but in the switchblade fight scene with Dean in *Rebel*, your reaction while he fights is terror, for him, and . . . love. Were you in love with James Dean?

He was a shitheel, sometimes. He liked being that way. But everybody had moments when they loved him—one way or another. I did, too. Did we have an affair, you mean?

Then, or perhaps later . . . ?

I might tell you some people I had affairs with—maybe. But Jimmy was special, so I don't want to say.

It's rare that a star has an affair with a star, isn't it?

It is, for the most part. Why do you think?

Why? Egos, I guess. It's easier to seduce or impress a fan than a costar.

You got it, kid. Also, there's that competitive thing: Who's the bigger star, the top man? A pun, again. *(Laughs.)*

Do you prefer fans or stars or starlets of either gender?

What do I prefer . . . Not stars, whatever that is. I mean, most people say I'm a star, but I know I'm not a superstar. Doesn't matter. I like real people, men who are happy being what they are, even if they don't earn a lot. I like English guys, because they got good manners and they're not so star-struck.

Blond Englishmen, huh?

Not necessarily blond, and not necessarily English. I like them all—men, I mean. And a few chicks, now and then.

Are you of a monogamous nature?

Make that polygamous, and you got it, kid. (*Smiles.*)

James Dean and Nick Adams were roommates, as I'm sure you know. Were they also lovers?

I didn't hear it from Jimmy, who was sort of awesome to me when we did *Rebel*. But Nick told me they had a big affair—I don't know if it was while they were living together or not. But there's always the roomie thing in Hollywood—Brando and Wally Cox, Brando and Tony Curtis, Cary Grant and Randolph Scott—and there are always rumors about them, even if they aren't true. . . I think Hollywood secretly *wants* to think it's true.

Why?

To some straight guys—straight execs, anyway—it's a way of tearing a star down to size. Envying him but despising him; that kind of thing—real twisted.

You said earlier you'd mention an affair you had with someone famous. For instance?

For instance? How about Peter Lawford?

Bi, right? How about Peter Lawford?

Yeah. (*Smiles.*) How about Peter Lawford. That's enough name-dropping for now. And I don't go much for groupies, either. Stars—big stars—*or* groupies; I like someone I can relate to like a kind of equal, you know?

So your ego has its limits?

Yeah. I'm basically a good guy. (*Smiles.*)

Was your bisexuality a problem, as far as your family was concerned, Sal?

As long as you don't wear a dress or sound like Marilyn Monroe, there's no problem that can't be worked out. One time, when my Ma wondered how come I turned out gay, I asked her, "Ma, how come my brothers *didn't*?" You get me?

Yeah—it's *there* to begin with.

You're catching on. Besides, when you're successful, you're *okay*, you know? Moms love success.

She must be proud you didn't change your name to Sal Miller or something.

She is. Imagine me, Sal Maynard—someone did suggest that.

Reminds me of Maynard G. Krebs.

(Both laugh.) He looked more like Maynard G. Crabs.

What about doing more television?

I did TV, way back when, and much more recently, and I could go that route. Only, how many shows can you guest on? I wouldn't mind my own show, but I'm not old or craggy enough to play a detective. Not yet. I'll probably do more of it, though.

What about directing TV?

Closed shop, pretty much. And no controversy allowed. I could play maybe a priest. . . . You know something? TV's so fuckin' old-fashioned and scared, but it's TV that got movies more liberal. TV and some gutsy guys like Preminger. To compete with TV, movies had to get more sexy and provocative, so TV made movies like *Rebel* possible. And that started the whole ball rolling. But TV itself is still for a kiddie version of the average working man.

You ought to go in there and stir things up.

Man, I'd like to stir things up.

Sal spent the night in town, at a motel on State Street, in front of West Beach. He called me the next morning, said he'd enjoyed talking together, and noted that he was spending the afternoon visiting an actress friend, before flying back to L.A. Eventually I found out that the friend was the ailing Norma Varden. A veteran of countless films, including *Witness for the Prosecution, The Sound of Music,* and *Doctor Dolittle,* the Englishwoman often went downtown to lunch, shop, or visit the museum of art. I'd met her in a supermarket, and she was extremely nice. But lately she hadn't been out and about. A dedicated Santa Barbaran, Ms. Varden continued to live there until poor health forced a move to the motion picture home in Los Angeles.

I never saw Sal Mineo again.

When he died, Sal was rehearsing for the L. A. opening of *P. S. Your Cat Is Dead.* He'd already played the bisexual cat burglar in the San Francisco production. Had he lived, I'd definitely have gone to see him at the Westwood Playhouse. I was stunned when I read that he had been stabbed to death on February 12, 1976, in front of his apartment house. He'd habitually walked to and from work. He didn't fear the dark, and had no known enemies.

Though his cinematic heyday had ended in the early sixties, Sal made headlines with his sudden death. Speculation abounded as to *why.* His sex life provided the unofficial but widely circulated answer. It was hinted that he was an S&M devotee, into bondage and other kinks. Or that he'd made a pass at a hustler and thus "provoked" his murderer—this, despite the multitude of gay hustlers to be found on West Hollywood's Santa Monica Boulevard. It was also loudly whispered that Sal Mineo's executioner might have been a former lover.

It wasn't the first time Sal had been the object of such ignorant speculations and malicious fantasizing. Part of the James Dean legend had it that his younger costar "turned queer" after Dean's untimely death in 1955. According to the story, Sal attempted fruitlessly to contact his fallen friend at a séance. He thereafter wrecked his car in an accident, but fate intervened to spare Sal's life. However, the words "James Dean" suddenly appeared on the car's windshield, and from that moment on, Sal Mineo was gay.

The yellow journalism surrounding Sal's death was fueled by the grisly murders of silent superstar Ramon Novarro and Italian director and intellectual Pier Paolo Pasolini. Novarro, the original Ben-Hur and a lover of Valentino, had died at the hands of two hustler brothers in 1968, in his own home. Pasolini, an ardent leftist with many enemies, was bludgeoned to death near Rome on November 3, 1975, just months before Sal died. His death caused a governmental scandal, and a likely murderer was quickly produced —some said too quickly.

Unlike Pasolini's mystery, Mineo's was eventually solved. It turned out that the thief who'd killed him had happened upon an innocent bystander. That the bystander was gay and an ex–movie star was a coincidence. Only after he was caught and jailed did the murderer learn that his victim had been Sal Mineo. The solution to the mystery was virtually ignored by the press.

Years after Sal's death, I met a Northern California restaurateur who'd been one of Sal's lovers while living in L.A. The ash-blond had recently arrived from England, and was taken by friends to Studio One, a large gay disco frequented by numerous gay actors, including Sal. Greg recalls, "He sent a friend over to me. The chap asked if I'd like to meet a movie star. I said 'Who?' He said, 'Sal Mineo.' I didn't know who Sal Mineo was, and the chap became irritated. 'Don't you ever watch television?' he asked. I said I was from Torquay, England. At any rate, I danced with Sal and then went to his apartment, whose walls were covered with photographs of famous people Sal had met. And we began our affair."

Greg knew Sal in 1974 and 1975. "We broke up because, although we had an open arrangement, Sal was rather possessive. And I was very young, slim and attractive, and I wanted to roam, to move on to other relationships, meet more people. But he was a nice guy—of Hollywood, but not *Hollywood.*" Greg offers these recollections of Sal Mineo:

"Back in the fifties, Sal played a character called Nicky on Ann Sothern's TV series. I saw one of those episodes—Nicky falls in love with 'a very lovely young girl'; but, by definition, girls are young . . . Sal said he'd had a fight with the show's director, about diction . . . One time, after dining in West Hollywood, we went back to my apartment and watched television. 'I Love Lucy' was on. Sal loved 'I Love Lucy.'

"Lucy was pronouncing things like *stew* 'styew' and *decided* 'dee—cided.' Being from England, I commented on it. Sal said he'd once met Joan Crawford, who'd had the nerve to criticize his diction—things like saying 'muthah.' Sal was sensitive about that, and about his family's early poverty. But Lucy and Crawford and all the old stars were taught to talk veddy clipped, which is why

Bette Davis sounds more English than I do. Anyway, Crawford turned Sal off, but she went on and on about the old studio days—she loved to talk about her 'starry self,' he said.

"Crawford mentioned a late superstar actor who was 'as gay as a goose,' and who was married off by his studio to a superstar actress who was also 'as gay as a goose,' an expression Sal hated. I asked why he didn't like it, and he said he couldn't stand farm animals. One couldn't tell if he was joking. I wanted to ask if he disliked animals in general, but thought better of it. I love animals, and we hadn't had sex yet, that evening.

"So I asked if Sal had ever taken diction lessons. I knew it might rub him the wrong way—so I could rub him the right way! He said the Sothern show's director had brought in a vocal coach, and after five minutes, Sal walked off the set. Sal also had a run-in with an anti-gay crew assistant. Don't ask me how the chap *knew*, way back then, though Sal once said he used to camp a lot, when he was younger. He was quite butch when I knew him, and quite out of the closet. I admired Sal as an up-front gay man, of which we have hardly any in England.

"Sal survived the episode. He was proud of being 'a survivor,' and according to him, he'd had a very rough childhood. He said he'd always known he was gay, but he only became sexual after getting involved in fisticuffs. Street fighting was a sex substitute, and the more he fought, the more he craved sexual contact. . . . It's ironic that he often played passive roles, because Sal was *not* sexually passive.

"Once he told me that he'd met the late Robert Taylor in Italy, in the mid sixties. Taylor was in decline. He was doing an Italian picture set in Egypt [*The Glass Sphinx*, (1967)]. And Sal knew he was gay. Taylor wasn't his type, but he craved his affection or approval. They were introduced, and went to a restaurant together, for drinks. It never got past drinks, because Taylor was—to Sal's dismay—not a friendly man. Not a 'buddy,' or a buddy to gays.

"Sal had heard gossip about Taylor, but it must have left out his politics. He was a long-time conservative who was ready to put down gays and liberals in public. He had denounced several suspected radicals during the fifties witch-hunts. I wonder that he even got together with Sal, because when Sal confided his own gayness—which no doubt Taylor had heard about—Taylor became very cold. He said he didn't wish to discuss politics. Sal hadn't

mentioned politics, but I suppose that to Taylor, coming out—
though just to another gay—was political.

"Sal went to the john, and when he came back, Taylor said he
had another engagement to rush off to. Sal wondered if Taylor
wasn't anti-ethnic, because Sal was proud of his heritage, but sensitive. Between being one of the few Italian-American actors who'd
kept his name, and being known in Hollywood as gay, he was
often suspicious of strangers. He'd opened up to Taylor, and been
swatted down. I knew it hurt him a lot. He asked me, 'How could
anyone with hair that dark be a bigot?'

"Sal was friends with Peter Bogdanovich before Bogdanovich
was a top director. He'd only directed something with Boris Karloff.
And one of Sal's biggest dissappointments was that Bogdanovich
hadn't given him the chance for a comeback in *The Last Picture
Show*. Because it was Sal who gave him a copy of the novel and
told him it would make a wonderful movie. Bogdanovich thanked
him repeatedly, but didn't give him a part.

"Eventually Sal knew he was through in pictures. He hadn't
achieved the transition to adult stardom. So he finally chucked
Hollywood. By the time he was in rehearsals for *P.S. Your Cat Is
Dead*, we'd stopped dating, but we kept in touch. One of my friends
stayed friends with Sal, and he told me that Sal was having more
fun with plays, working honestly and creatively, than he'd ever
had in Hollywood. It didn't mean so much to me then. But it did
after his death.

"Sal would have hated that the robber [Sal's murderer] didn't
know who he was! As for all the scandal coverage, he'd probably
have been amused. Sal never cared much what the public or the
neighbors thought. His peers' approval was what counted. He
wanted less to be a star than to do good work and be acknowledged
as a craftsman. He played hard, worked very hard, and he still
had a lot of potential. . . ."

Luchino Visconti
1906–1976

ABOUT a month after Sal Mineo's death, in a setting less Felliniesque than L.A., Luchino Visconti died amid Roman splendor. Unlike the struggling immigrant Mineos, the Viscontis were aristocrats through and through. Posters all over Rome proclaimed national "pain and grief" on behalf of the "man of culture" renowned throughout Europe. The funeral on March 19 was attended by, among others, President Giovanni Leone and Burt Lancaster.

Luchino, one of the Duke of Modrone's seven offspring, distinguished himself as perhaps the most famous of his line. The Viscontis descended from King Desiderius, Charlemagne's father-in-law. Luchino's mother was a famous beauty whose ancestors were noted by Napoleon. His father was an acclaimed musician whose forebears had once ruled Lombardy, then become *signori* in pre-Renaissance Milano, where they thrived and domineered; one fourteenth-century Visconti became known as the Viper of Milano, and figures in a novel by Marjorie Bowen.

Himself a renaissance man, Luchino Visconti was best known as a director of such controversial classics as *The Leopard, Death in Venice, La Terra Trema, Rocco and His Brothers,* and *The Damned.* Before Luchino could speak, he was being taken to some of Milano's forty-odd cinemas. He virtually "grew up in La Scala," where the Viscontis owned a personally decorated box. And his musically and culturally astute father presented the youth with copies of Proust. Luchino's interests and films reflected this culturally sumptuous background. Along the way, the *maestro*'s eye for beauty— and sometimes talent—made a star of protégé Alain Delon, turned friend Dirk Bogarde from "England's Loretta Young" into a re-

28

spected dramatic actor, and starred his final, openly bisexual protégé Helmut Berger in various costly, semi-uncloseted movie spectaculars.

In August 1975 I was in Venice, having worked my way southward from London. While in the city of watery boulevards, I paid my respects at Diaghilev's resting place on San Michele, the mortuary island, with its hundreds of miniature lizards. I also met my friend Enrico Zanghi, an Italian journalist, who informed me that in a few weeks the *maestro* would begin filming anew—from a wheelchair. In 1972, while filming *Ludwig*, a lavish biography of Germany's mad, bad emperor, Visconti was felled "by lightning." The stroke rendered his left arm useless. During the first few weeks of recuperation in a Zurich sanitarium, Visconti was incapacitated. The fate of the multimillion dollar *Ludwig* hung in the balance.

The director had been warned that he was overworking himself and smoking too heavily—often a hundred cigarettes a day. He'd blithely ignored his doctors' advice, and, following the stroke, it was feared Visconti might lapse into a coma. But within the month, he was able to sit up. He regained his normal functions, and eventually he could walk with a cane. Within two months, he was completing *Ludwig*. The following year he did another Berger-starrer, *Conversation Piece*. Unable to walk without the detested cane, Visconti had to move from his Roman manse to a villa in the Papal resort of Castel Gandolfo (near Rome), because of the required in-house elevators.

L'Innocente, made in 1975, was his final film. Zanghi arranged for me an interview with Visconti that September, at the Hotel Villa La Principessa, a park hotel at Lucca, near Florence. The cast—headed by Giancarlo Giannini and Laura Antonelli—and crew were domiciled at La Principessa; on November 2, they helped the master celebrate his sixty-ninth and last birthday there. He held a press conference and declared, "Here I am, ready to make *another* film, even if I do need a wheelchair. Next time it will be a stretcher, but I shall never give up."

Despite spontaneous bursts of Mediterranean warmth, the man with the eagle profile and disconcertingly hawklike intensity wasn't easy to interview. He was an intimidating figure. And a tired one who husbanded most of his strength for moviemaking. Before our two evening sessions began, he reminded me that he'd agreed to speak with me on condition that I not probe into his private life or dwell on his left-wing politics, which he knew were anathema to most Americans. Excepting an occasional word or phrase, communication wasn't a problem, and alternated between English and Italian. I'd been reared with English, Spanish, and French; my father, who studied at the Sorbonne, once taught at the American University of Beirut, and my mother was a beauty queen and alpinist from Mexico City. In college, and after, I studied German and Italian.

Thanks to a claustrophobic stint in a library in Florence, I came prepared with pertinent questions and observations. (I was already a fan of particular Visconti films.) I wasn't prepared, however, for the energetic staccato of Visconti's conversation. Several times during our sessions, the director smilingly paused and assured me that if I had any need of reiteration or clarification, I could ask his assistant afterward, at our leisure.

My questions aren't in chronological order. . . .

Ah . . . Let's talk, now.

Good. Let's talk about two of the most important women in your life, Maria Callas and Coco Chanel. Perhaps Callas first.

What do you want to know?

Well, something that always comes to mind with Callas is the way she went from heavy to virtually sylphlike.

Yes. She remade herself and her career, with unbelievable determination.

Audrey Hepburn has always been one of my favorites. I understand that she served as an inspiration for Callas.

Absolutely, she did. She was her icon. You are too young to remember, but in the 1950s that actress had a great influence on how women in Europe and America wanted to look. It was more realistic for them to become like her than like Marilyn Monroe!

What finally led her to do it?

Callas? She admired Miss Hepburn in *Roman Holiday*, and from then on she taped her photographs to her walls, in the kitchen, everywhere. She almost starved herself. Of course *then* she could play almost anything she chose—which did not mean that she still wasn't taking great risks, artistically. Callas thought communicating was the most important thing, and she always took a risk, to communicate her own vision.

You've directed her in various operas, including *Traviata* and *Anna Bolena*. Was she ever a prima donna?

In Italian it means "first lady." She is that. Playing a courtesan—a prostitute, after all—she brought back the beauty and elegance which were originally the mark of a royal *courtisane*. She breathed new life into *Traviata*, and I was as familiar with *Traviata* as a child is with his cherished plaything.

I haven't seen many operas, but I did read somewhere that you caused a scandal by having Callas, as Violetta, kick her shoes off.

Yes! *Then.* Now . . . *(Shrugs.)* It is thought to be well and good.

Why would removing her shoes provoke such intense reaction?

Men don't usually like to see a woman's feet. Unlike in China. *(Laughs.)*

But in China, the foot was considered very sexual and arousing, and was bared only between lovers.

And Violetta and Alfredo were lovers. . . .

Can you comment on Callas's relationship with Onassis?

Not for publication, and not in conversation, either. She is a very private lady. [Callas was then still alive; she died in 1977.]

You've had a hand in the look of all the operas, plays, and films you've done . . .

You see, a *maestro* conducts, arranges the elements into a whole. . . . It also means an instructor, but I do not teach those I work with, although hopefully something is taught to the audience.

You've been described as an impatient man. In what way?

How am I impatient? I hate to waste the time. To be idle is not to live.

You were also close to Chanel, weren't you?

She took me in her hand and helped me to meet people who would teach me and help me. I adored her, of course.

What in particular did you two have in common?

A love of beauty and using it in our work, we had. And also we loved racehorses. I still do, but now I can't . . . (*Gestures sadly and impatiently.*) Chanel could not have lived in a wheelchair.

I understand you used a cane, before.

I hated that! The doctors say I don't pay attention. They're right! (*Laughs.*) I didn't want to continue with the cane. So I exercised, but too much. I *fell.* (*Sighs.*) Then I lost the cane and gained the wheelchair.

Chanel was your confidante, wasn't she?

Yes. And she played mother confessor. She consoled me. Many, many times.

You knew her in the thirties?

Yes. In 1935 I was asked to England by Gabriel Pascal, the director—the man who worked with Shaw. But nothing happened, and it was a big unhappiness for me. A false turn. Chanel consoled me. But one of the best things she did for me was to introduce me to Jean Renoir.

She knew everyone, didn't she?

Sometimes, my boy, she seemed to *be* everyone. She lived life so fully, she did so many things. And she knew all the leading figures of art and fashion because her own situation was unparalleled, especially for a female.

Who did Renoir introduce you to?

Most importantly, he was a master of cinema. Of course, from his father, Auguste Renoir, he knew much about art—he knew by experiencing it in daily life, as I did. When you grow up with artists, it colors the outlook.

Did Renoir *fils* also color your political outlook?

Everyone knows he was always surrounded with political people, including many Communists.

Why was Marxism so attractive to young people in the 1930s?

It . . . it offered hope. And remember, it was long before Hungary, 1956, or Czechoslovakia, 1968. It had not betrayed itself so publicly.

Yet Stalin was purging right and left. It's amazing to realize that he killed even more people than Hitler.

That is *now* known. . . .

So Renoir was a mentor too.

Yes. He was like a brother.

To whom else did Chanel introduce you?

To Paris! I went to Paris, but she made a pilgrimage of it.

You also went to Hollywood in the thirties. I envy you that!

Another pilgrimage. But of course, I *knew*, beforehand. From the cinema. Nineteen . . . thirty-seven. *Camille*, I had just seen. *La divina Garbo!* (*Metaphorically kisses his fingers.*) Then I meet Signor Cukor, the great director, and I ask him how is Miss Garbo. And that is all. . . . (*Throws hands upward and shrugs tragicomically.*) I did not ask the thousand and one questions, because as a future movie director, I did not want him to think I was just a fan.

You met Garbo later, though?

Yes. But much later. . . .

What did you think of George Cukor?

A very nice man, and genial. Perhaps because he was fat. I like fat people. A wonderful director, of course, as everyone knows.

When did you meet Garbo, and where?

We met more than once. But until I was older, I could not make a real conversation with someone like her. (*Mock-slaps forehead.*) *Mascalzone!* There *is* no one like Garbo.

It would have been interesting to watch Garbo portray Chanel.

Maybe . . . But both had elegance.

What did you think of Valentino—the *actor*? I've never heard what an Italian thinks of Rudolph Valentino.

I don't know if I am typical, or if my answer will be typical. . . . Eh, he was interesting. But not as interesting as the women around him, especially the artistic lesbians. One of them [Alla Nazimova] participated in the film of *Salomé*, from Oscar Wilde, with all the *look* inspired by Beardsley. In 1967 when I directed *another Traviata*, at Covent Garden, I did an *hommage* to England by using Beardsley as my inspiration. The sets and costumes were descendants of *The Yellow Book*.

I never saw Valentino's first big picture, *The Four Horsemen of the Apocalypse*, which made him an overnight star. But I saw the remake, starring Glenn Ford, and I wish I hadn't. Did *you* see that?

Yes, yes. It was very good. How strange—all the Americans seemed to hate it. It was ignored in America, which is the worst way to hate a movie. But Minnelli did a fine job, I thought. It was popular in Europe.

But *Glenn Ford*?

True, very true. The *studio*, no doubt. I know that Minnelli wanted Delon.

You made a star of Delon. . . .

It would have happened anyway. . . . Such an attractive boy.

Is Delon the handsomest actor you've worked with?

I have worked with many beautiful young men. *(Smiles.)*

Are they lesser actors than plainer men?

. . . Usually. Because they have not had the same big well of emotion and suffering to draw up from. Your blond California surfer boys appear to have no depth whatever. . . .

The sea beneath them has depth. *(Both laugh.)* What was young Delon like? You made a star of him in *Rocco*. . . .

He loved to work. It gave him a purpose. He'd escaped from home and gone to fight in Vietnam, before the Americans got there.

When it was still called Indochina. Then he had different little jobs, until he and the cinema discovered each other . . . He is an appreciative young man, very respectful, but we have not worked together for a long time. . . .

You've traveled extensively, haven't you?

One loves to travel. But not now. Today it is a mass assembly-line business. Everywhere the crowds, the ropes to prevent vandals, and in Italy, so much terrorism. When I traveled, it was altogether different. It was something of leisure and beauty. There were few tourists.

But now culture is accessible to more people. . . .

So you have more tourists. What do most of them achieve? They take the photographs, buy something for the women to wear, then go home to America and say that this other country was very different from America!

And they often draw the most negative comparisons.

Not only Americans, of course. But most tourists go to feel like Gulliver in a land of quaint, charming, *little* things.

I understand you had a villa in Ischia.

A very beautiful island. Mystical. Small towns, very tranquil, very private beaches.

I've always wanted to visit Ischia, Sardinia, and Pompeii.

Then someday you will. . . . Pompeii, you want to see the ruins?

Yeah, I've always been very interested in archaeology, reading about Champollion, Carter, Winckelmann. . . .

Johann Winckelmann. Yes. . . . He worked at Pompeii. You know he was homosexual, no?

Winckelmann? Really? No . . . I guess these things don't get into biographies. Did . . . you didn't know him?

(*Laughs.*) No, no. But it is well known here that he died in Trieste—a violent young . . . a companion for the night.

A hustler?

Sì, sì. Chi sa? [Who knows?] Maybe one of them says, *"Vuoi che ti succhio?"* [Do you want me to suck you?] and the other agrees, and—*pouf!* He is gone, dead, life is over. Is not always worth it, sex, if it brings on death.

Johann Winckelmann, huh? I'm amazed. Thank you for telling me.

It does not alter your view of the man, eh?

Not at all. Just makes him seem a bit more colorful, or interesting . . . Have you been to San Michele, in Venice?

Diaghilev? Of course. You see the lizards? Yes? You have a picnic?

Certamente—or *certo.* . . .

Both are correct. What did you eat?

French bread, I mean, *pane*, and *parmigiano*—which sure beats the Parmesan back home. It was interesting that it isn't sold by the pound or kilo or whatever, but by the *etto*. That's an Italian measure, isn't it?

Yes and no; it means . . . hec-to-gram: *ettogrammo*. What else did you eat there?

I got some *dolci ebraici* [Hebrew pastries] near the Venice train station. . . . Delicious—with white powdered sugar, you know.

Sei ebreo? [You are Jewish?]

Yes, partly. . . . And you?

Partly—in sympathy. Long, long ago, I was in the anti-Fascist movement.

I know—in World War II.

But . . . *(Shrugs sadly.)* It is not over. Still, there are bombings of anti-Fascist meetings, and so on. Enough, though, about politics.

Has the life of Diaghilev ever interested you as a cinematic subject? He had such a rich, rounded life, so pivotal to the arts in this century.

Assolutamente! His life should be put onto the screen, but it is now for someone else to do. Even to do Nijinsky, I was not able. For years, I wanted to do that film, with Nureyev as Nijinsky.

It's not too late, is it?

For me, or for Rudi?

Either.

No. It *is* too late, for both. Nijinsky was very young when he was with Diaghilev and the Ballets Russes.

Who would you have wanted to portray Diaghilev?

Brando. Always, one wants Brando—for everything, one wants him. . . .

But I can't see Brando doing a Russian accent.

Probably not. If Diaghilev is ever on the screen, I think it will be by an Englishman, and . . . no accent. [Herbert Ross's 1980 *Nijinsky* featured an accentless Alan Bates.]

You've also sought Brando for *Remembrance of Things Past*?

I seek to make the movie of Proust, but always problems . . . If it had been ready, I would want Brando for Charlus. [The 1984 *Swann's Way* costarred Alain Delon as Baron de Charlus.] But it is too late now.

Surely not.

No, I know. It *is*. . . .

Having lived so long in Rome, did you get to visit every museum there? I don't think any traveler could ever accomplish that.

Not every one. *(Smiles.)* You like museums and the old things in them?

Not everything in them is antiquated. I saw my first erection in a Roman museum.

A guard?!

No. It was in the Vatican Museum, in 1967. With my family; my dad was on sabbatical, so we had eight months abroad.

Very educational . . .

You're telling me. But anyway, they'd gone on ahead, from one room of statuary—Greco-Roman—to another. I was two rooms behind them. And at the end of one room, a male nude. . . . But it looked funny, from afar, because of the piece of marble, protruding. Especially since most of the male nudes in the Vatican were covered with a fig-leaf. So—I was alone in the room; as you say, far fewer crowds then—I approached. And it was an erection, and I'd never seen one before.

You were how old?

I'd just turned thirteen the week before, in Athens. And I'd seen more than my share of statues, like in Paris, where most American tourists are shocked by all the penises.

But it is amazing you had never seen an erection on a real boy.

No, because I'd only been in junior high for one month, and in the gym's shower room, there was nudity, of course, but no erections. And then in October we left for New York and Europe.

And not your own?

You mean . . . ? You know, looking back, I'm amazed how unaware I was, then, of my own body. The *mental* things were stressed. . . .

Did you ask a guard what the statue was—from where?

I wouldn't have dared, at the time. And there weren't anywhere as many guards as there are now.

You have never seen erotic Greek vases?

No. I've known they exist—heterosexual and homosexual— but I guess they keep them locked up, or they've been destroyed already.

If you were in Italy longer, I could arrange for you to see some. *(Winks.)* Most are of men, together. Very explicit, but very artistic. . . . The Church hides what it has not ruined. It is surprising you saw the erection statue where you did.

I know, but it's absolutely true. Years later, a history teacher in high school said there's a room in the Vatican Museum containing all the remaining organs which the fig-leaves had covered. . . . I don't suppose the statue is there now—probably. [It wasn't, in 1983.]

You are going on to Rome?

Not this time, Signor Visconti. No time left. . . . But you're completing *The Intruder* [*L'Innocente*] in Rome, aren't you?

Yes, yes. I will finish it at Cinecittà, and maybe it will finish me. *(Smiles wryly.)*

Speaking of ancient history, haven't you wanted to make a costume picture set in Roman or Greek times?

Sì . . . Sì. But it is expensive, and it can be done better on the stage now. The Roman epics, now even Hollywood does not make them, so we no longer hear the old Romans talking with English accents! *(Laughs.)* But in the time of silent movies, *Italy* made wonderful epics—the *big* ones, with huge sets, and Hollywood learned from *us*.

Like the silent *Ben-Hur* with Ramon Novarro?

Oh, yes! *(Kisses fingers lustily.)* Much more excitement than the one Signor Wyler made a few years ago [with Charlton Heston].

Isn't it terrible, the way he died?

They should have executed the two criminals. . . .

Does Renaissance culture interest you more than, say, ancient Greek culture?

Because of my family and its history, I am always intrigued by the medieval and Renaissance and more recent times. But . . . all history . . . and with the sexual climate of ancient Greece, it is always worth studying. And so beautiful; do you know that in ancient Greek there was no word for homosexuality? Because there is just . . . to be *sexual.* One is not this or that, one is *sexual.*

But even though some say that bisexuality is the norm, or would be without religious and social taboos, don't you think everyone has a primary, a dominant, sexual orientation?

Oh, yes. Not a choice, but an instinct.

I've never met a fifty-fifty bisexual. Have you?

No. Always, there is . . . a dominance. But sometimes it takes many years to realize which it is.

It probably did, years back. I think today's kids are aware of their dominant sexuality earlier.

Yes. But it can take time. . . .

You were engaged to a princess once?

There was . . . an expectation of marriage. Very long ago. Not a formal engagement, and nothing exceptionally interesting there. Please ask me anything you like. . . .

You worked with one of Diaghilev's associates . . . ?

You mean Nicola Benois? Of course he was the son of Aleksandr, who did create wonderful scenery for the Ballets Russes.

What do you think of the Italian-American actors, starting with Brando?

Brando is unique. But, not through his own fault, he gets too much credit in America. Because the rebellious trend in American movie acting began not with him, *ma* with Clift. *Then* came Brando and James Dean, and the others . . . There are many good young actors in America, some of them of Italian *origin.*

Which of them would you like to work with?

Pacino. Brando, obviously. Bancroft, Anne Bancroft—of Italian origin . . . De Niro is interesting. There are many good actors, and I do not make national categories. . . .

You don't work in Hollywood much. . . .

Of course not. I am more interested in art, even if this sounds arrogant.

The Hollywood mentality is money first, right?

Money and the bogus morality. Not just about *gay* things; about anything they do not like or understand. Always, they want to lower the picture, to make it pleasing to the most uneducated man in the smallest town in the most faraway state.

You had trouble making *Death in Venice,* with its homosexual theme?

The theme is not only homosexual, but there *is* homosexuality. Although no sex at all. Still, Hollywood wanted me to change the *boy* to a *girl!* They do not even *know* of Thomas Mann! *(Gestures hopelessly.)*

I understand that Warners helped finance *Death* because your previous film, *The Damned*, was such a big hit.

Yes, very popular. In Europe, above all. American television, another situation. . . .

I remember that! There was a hubbub about the title; for a while, it looked like it would be *The Bleeped*. It was shown at 11:30—I stayed up to watch it. I'll never forget Helmut Berger's Dietrich imitation, at the opening.

But you did not see *La Caduta degli Dei* [*The Damned*, a.k.a *Götterdämmerung*]. What you saw was bowdlerized. The Night of the Long Knives, they thought it was immoral and "insignificant," one censor said! So, they make . . . *(Makes scissoring gesture.)*

Still, *The Damned* made money, and so did *Death in Venice* . . .

It *still* almost did not get to be made! Many difficulties. Then the studio secretly decided to make it into an official loss, which they do in America after spending millions of dollars. I complained: I told them I would make an international scandal and tell all the newspapers . . . Eh, *bene*. So, finally, it was ready. And—in Europe—popular with everyone.

And particularly popular in Japan. . . .

In Japan, homosexual—no: homoerotic—relationships are common. There is the cult of the *bishonen*, the beautiful young man who must die in his full glory. Or who brings with him death— an angel of death. So the movie is still showing there, and still the mail comes. It made me popular there; in Japan, for one special movie, they can admire you.

Bjorn Andresen, the blond Swede whom you cast as Tadzio, didn't want to be in the picture?

He wanted a big Honda! *(Laughs.)* He wanted the biggest, best motorcycle! So he let his grandmama bring him to see me in Stockholm, where I was casting—I went all over Scandinavia, to look, after the newspapers announced me. I found Bjorn immediately. I knew *he* was Tadzio—the "hyacinth curls" of which Mann wrote. But I did the tour, so as not to disappoint the hopeful ones. But of course I cast Tadzio—no, no: *Bjorn*. Bjorn.

When you offered the lead to Dirk Bogarde, he said it was better than being asked to play Hamlet by Olivier.

Bogarde is my good friend. We have had—how do you say?—our ups . . . but only one down. . . . That was when I wanted him to play in *Gruppo di Famiglia in un Interno* [*Conversation Piece*]. Never mind; Burt Lancaster played the professor, and *better*.

That also costarred Helmut Berger, right?

Ma, sì . . . (Shrugs quizzically.) But—what were we talking about first?

Dirk Bogarde in *Death in Venice*.

What did you want to ask me?

Well, he was in *The Damned*, first. And . . . his role was cut?

Ah . . . Originally, I wanted a Macbeth story of this family, like the Krupps. I did want Vanessa Redgrave too [as Sophie], but Ingrid Thulin was marvelous instead. I wanted to show the turning point where the choice to be fascistic became no longer a choice—it became irreversible. Through the family structure of the fictional von Essenbecks, I show this.

You've often used families as social microcosms. Because of your own lineage, do families interest you particularly?

Yes, yes. It is the basic structure in society. And it is always in conflict, so it is good for the movie plot. But . . . oh, so as I am editing all the hours and hours of film, I see that the story has to . . . *shift*. To a story of corrupted youth. So Berger, who plays the son of Sophie [Thulin], becomes the center. You see how he is corrupted, he is offered power, by the Nazi character, who is Helmut Griem.

He was great in *Cabaret*, where he played the bisexual baron.

Excuse me?

You saw *Cabaret*? Griem was a non-Nazi in it, but being sup-

posedly bisexual, he's the agent who nearly corrupts Michael York, along with Liza Minnelli. Did you like *Cabaret?*

Yes, very full of atmosphere, but . . . *(Shakes head from side to side.)* You know, don't you, the story is from the novel of Christopher Isherwood? The York one, he is based on the author. So the integrity of the sex . . . is not really there.

It's a semicloseted film. But the original, in the 1950s, was totally closeted. I haven't seen that one, it's never on TV.

Who was in it?

Laurence Harvey and . . . Julie Harris. It's hard to see her as Sally Bowles.

No, she is a good actress.

Yes, very good, but not the type one thinks of. You know, you say that *Cabaret* is sexually dishonest, but your own pictures have been less than bold, in terms of gay characters, although gay relationships are often *implied.*

You think *so*. You are young: impatient.

You're impatient too, Maestro—if I may call you Maestro. . . .

Thank you. *(Bows head slightly.)* You think I am old-fashioned?

Not old-fashioned. But . . . you're not, as they say, in the closet very much; I mean, it's known in Europe that you are a gay artist. *(He smiles at the word "gay.")* And you're daring enough to include and insist on—as in *Death in Venice* and *The Damned*—gay . . . *themes.* But you always stop short.

How? *(Peers intently.)*

Well, I don't know—there's a sort of flirting with gayness. In *The Damned,* there are beautiful male bodies, there's transvestism, yet . . . not one gay character. Except, maybe—fleetingly—in some of the Long Knives sequence. I did see *The Damned* at a campus screening, in California.

You are right. The villain—Berger—if you want to call him the real villain, he is not homosexual.

But when it came out, in America, most of the critics denounced the homosexuality in the film, and most talked about . . . Martin? as if he were *gay*.

Silly people.

John Simon always takes the opportunity of reviewing your films to denounce gays and your own . . . sexuality. What do you think of critics like Simon, or Pauline Kael, or even the less homophobic ones?

They are not creators. And being critics, they do not love art. I have no time for them.

Then, since you asked, in films like *Death in Venice* and *Conversation Piece*, you have older men in love with younger men, but always choosing to restrict themselves, smothering their sexuality and ultimately conforming in suffering.

How would you change this?

I'm not the filmmaker. But since you're honest, why not be . . . well, really honest?

In five, ten years, I hope there can be more honesty. But now, if I am honest, the way you want, my films cannot be shown in America.

That's not quite true. Look at *Sunday, Bloody Sunday*, which you championed at some film festival or other.

Ah . . . Now I am tired. *Tomorrow* I will tell you what you want to know about that movie—very good movie. But now, I have to go and rest until the morning. (*Turns to his assistant; they smile knowingly.*) One favor . . . (*Visconti's finger goes up.*) With your other questions, will you try to put them into order of chronology? It is difficult to answer about one, then go back in time, then jump to the future. You will do this? To help an old man. It makes more sense when it is unfolding like life. . . .

Buongiorno, Signor Visconti. Did you rest well?

Comme ci, comme ça. What did you do in Florence today?

Walked the Ponte Vecchio and looked in the shops there. . . .

Ate ice cream and sat in the Piazza della Signoria. There's no shortage of things to do and see.

What else did you do?

I put my questions—all the ones I could—into chronological order. . . .

Va bene. (Smiles.) But, what *else* did you do?

. . . I talked with Enrico—Mr. Zanghi—on the phone, and told him how well it went last night.

Who?

Signor Zanghi arranged this interview. . . .

Conversazione—is nicer. To meet someone nice and new is always good, it gives . . . energy.

I'm just glad we could meet and talk in person. That's rare with directors making a movie. This is much better than doing a phone interview.

Caro, we would not have done a "phone interview." I hate to be using the telephone . . . So what else do you have to tell me about your activities, eh? *(Smiles expectantly.)*

Well, really, not much. Writing letters home to explain why I've stayed on longer than I planned. But, Maestro, I'll tell you my stories, if you'll tell me yours. . . .

(Both smile.) Caro, at my age, there is little to tell.

Same here. You know what they say: all work and no play makes Giacomo a dull tourist. . . . Shall we begin at the beginning?

You didn't want me to tell you about *Sunday, Bloody Sunday*?

Sure, go ahead; please.

I liked it very much. Something to admire—the honesty and artistry. And so I tell everyone I like it, and I embrace my colleague, John Schlesinger.

It's interesting that, just as you were able to make *Death in*

Venice because of *The Damned's* success, Schlesinger has said that United Artists gave him *Sunday, Bloody Sunday* "as a present," after the huge success of *Midnight Cowboy.*

Yes. The American studios rarely but sometimes choose to finance something which will only earn them prestige. Now, do you have anything else to ask about this picture? No? Then we go back to the beginning.

Where were you born?

No, no, no! Not so far—I thought you want to ask about my movies.

Okay. I just have certain films I want to ask you about, and . . . other topics.

The films with English titles, yes? *(Smiles.)*

Some, yes. Tell me, who are your favorite authors?

Two authors I have always liked are Proust and Mann.

And your father actually gave you Proust, as a present?

Yes. And in those days, Proust was not the great classic of today. He was thought to be *new*, perhaps a trend. Many people disapproved. But my father thought it would be useful—somehow, he knew . . .

What actor or actors did you particularly admire as a youth?

Duse. But don't ask me to *tell* you about Duse—there is too much to tell. You have to read *books*, and even then, you will never *know* Duse.

Everyone says she was greater than Bernhardt. . . .

She lived for art . . .

The implication being that the divine Sarah lived for Sarah's divinity?

(Nods.) But I was also impressed by all the actors I saw in the cinemas, the many cinemas of Milano.

You learned German at an early age?

I had a German governess. Until World War I.

Did you have a crush on any movie stars?

Gary Cooper!

And in your youth, you met many of the great cultural figures. How?

Money . . . (*Smiles apologetically.*) And I had wonderful race-horses, so I traveled with them, to the races which we won—which *they* won.

I see you met Cocteau, Kurt Weill, some I've never heard of, Chanel of course, Franco Zeffirelli . . .

Ma . . . Franco, he was a bambino! Not yet a director. He was acting then. I put him into *Crime and Punishment*, which I directed.

You've directed numerous plays, and introduced many famous plays and playwrights to Italy, including Tennessee Williams and Arthur Miller.

But also I worked in Paris, doing plays.

Didn't Zeffirelli work with you behind the camera?

Oh, yes. *La Terra Trema* . . . he was one of my assistants.

He didn't act in that?

(*Reproving stare.*) All the characters in *La Terra Trema* were the local people—as *themselves*. You did not see it?

I'm afraid not. . . . The best pictures seldom get on television.

Not the ones in other languages. Who do they show on American television the most?

I think they go more by stars than directors. People like John Wayne, Jerry Lewis . . . or Rock Hudson or Elvis Presley—their movies are on often.

The *stars*, eh?

Evidently. What do you think of Zeffirelli the director?

A charming young man. Now very busy with movies, with opera. What do *you* think of his pictures?

I notice that the critics either ignore or dwell on the gay aspects of his movies.

Which aspects do you remember?

The bare-ass shots in *Romeo and Juliet* **and** *Brother Sun, Sister Moon,* **the swishy milliner in** *The Taming of the Shrew.*

So you think . . .

What?

About Franco . . . ?

That he's gay?

Of course. But do not print this.

Is it known in Italy?

They know . . . [Zeffirelli has since come out in *The Advocate.*]

You've worked with Dalí . . .

Scenery . . . Franco has also done magnificent scenery for me.

You did the Italian *Streetcar.* **What do you think of Tennessee Williams or Anna Magnani?**

I wanted Magnani for one movie, but she was pregnant. We worked together later. Tennessee Williams? Everything he did was revolutionary then. People talked and talked—they wanted to know if he was revolutionist or political, if he was just making a scandal to be shocking, or who knows.

You also did *Death of a Salesman,* **which is hard to visualize in a foreign tongue or setting.**

I did many, many plays. You do not want to go through them all?

Of course not. In one of your first films, you worked with Farley Granger—in *Senso.*

You very much like him?

Not particularly. I'm reminded, because earlier this year I saw a dancer named Tommy Tune, who resembles him, facially.

What—in what—you have seen Farley Granger?

Strangers on a Train, by Hitchcock, and a not so good one about some turn-of-the-century beauty [played by Joan Collins], called *The Girl in the Red Velvet Swing*. There's another pseudo-gay Hitchcock film with Granger, *Rope*, but it's out of circulation. [It was re-released after Hitchcock's death.]

Yes, he made some interesting roles. But in Italy, he is not too well known. You know?—I wanted Brando for the part, but Granger was good. I wanted Ingrid Bergman, but Alida Valli was good.

I suppose *Senso* was *after* the war in Ethiopia. . . .

Of course. Why?

Chronology?

(Laughs.) No, no, please don't worry. *(Smiles.)* I wanted to see if you take direction. . . . Ask me; ask me.

Was it the war in Ethiopia that firmed your resolve to fight Fascism?

I was anti-Fascist before then . . . but that . . . changed things.

And you were almost executed by the Fascists?

So were many other people. It was just an incident—in those days there were life-or-death incidents very often, throughout Italy.

I wasn't aware that Maximilian Schell's father was a famous Austrian poet and playwright.

The whole family is very special: Herman Karl, the father; the mother, an actress; the five children all actors—Maximilian, but also my friend Maria Schell. Do you like Max?

He certainly earned his Oscar in *Judgment at Nuremberg*. But he was also good in the movie of *Five Finger Exercise*, which was a flop, apparently.

Max is very intelligent, and also a good director. Someone who loves the arts, and we have much in common.

I read you wanted to make a documentary about Tibet?

It is fascinating, no? Its gentle religion, the Dalai Lama, the struggle with China before and after Communism, the continuation of the ancient culture. But this was long ago, and I did not get to do it—it was while the Dalai Lama still lived in Lhasa, in that magnificent temple-palace.

I saw a picture of your father, who was very handsome and resembled Gore Vidal, who lives in Ravello. Do you know Gore?

The entire world knows him, no? *(Smiles.)*

What makes you laugh, Maestro?

(Laughs.) Your question. Why do you ask it?

I think it's very revealing. Don't you?

It makes someone vulnerable, when you know.

More vulnerable than if you find out what makes someone cry, do you think?

Possibly . . . One can share tears, but to laugh, that is very individual. Comedy makes many responses, no? But tragedy . . .

What's your favorite of your own films?

The one I'm making now.

And after that?

The one I make after that?

No, I meant, other than this one, which is your favorite?

You tell me the one you think is your favorite.

Of the ones I've seen? I guess *Death in Venice*. I like Venice, Bogarde, Silvana Mangano . . . the music, of course.

You like Mahler?

Certainly.

(Beam s.) You have good taste. *Buon gusto* . . . You like the ending?

Of *Death in Venice*? It is downbeat . . . The poor guy dies, and he hardly even says hi to the young man.

The American money people also wanted me to change it.

I don't know that it should be changed; I didn't mean that. It does reflect its time period. The *world* was in the closet—gay, straight . . .

To give *you* an answer: I particularly like *Rocco e i Suoi Fratelli.*

You've worked with Carlo Ponti, but never with Sophia Loren—one of the few Italian directors who hasn't worked with her.

We came close . . . But Ponti, who is a typical hard-working Milanese, produced a picture [*Boccaccio '70*] in which I did one segment.

I like those portmanteau movies. But they never do well in America. . . . Didn't your segment star Romy Schneider?

Yes. A charming young lady. Very elegant. I introduced her to Chanel, who gave her good advice. . . .

Did that make her a star, then?

. . . It helped.

You also enhanced Burt Lancaster's reputation with *The Leopard.*

He came to me a star and a fine actor. And we became good friends. . . .

You wanted to film Mann's *The Magic Mountain*?

Mann is a lifelong fascination for me. A movie of his family's life would be wonderful. You are familiar with his children?

Erika Mann, the poet . . . She married W. H. Auden, didn't she?

As a political statement, and to move from under the Nazis into the light of England.

Auden was gay, of course.

So was Miss Mann. And her great brother Klaus, a writer and anti-Fascist. Do you know of him?

I'm afraid not. What did *he* write?

Mephisto. Pathetic Symphony, about Tchaikovsky . . .

I'll have to look him up in the library. But you never got close to financing *The Magic Mountain*? I would have thought West German investment outfits . . .

I came very close to getting the American finance for Proust. Olivier became a lord, so they thought he was acceptable as Charlus! *(Laughs wearily.)* But . . . no.

Were you disappointed by the commercial failure of *Ludwig*?

My boy, what do you mean?! It was not a failure, either with critics *or* audiences.

I guess I meant in America. . . .

A pity, of course. But America is one part of the audience, only. And we knew that *Ludwig* was mostly for Europeans.

Most Americans are only interested in *English* royalty. . . . You also wanted to do a movie about Zelda Fitzgerald?

For every picture I did, there were a dozen I wanted, and dreamed about making. Yes, Zelda, she interested me, as a wonderful character. And when I read her novel [*Save Me the Waltz*], I began to plan it. Like so many ladies who lived in the background of a man, she was more interesting than he was. You know what Scott, your great American novelist, said of his wife? You should *all* know this. "Possibly she would have been a genius if we had never met." Hmmm? *(Raises eyebrows quizzically.)*

A . . . real possibility. I don't know much about her, but I know Scott Fitzgerald was supposed to be very domineering . . . Did she write that novel before meeting him, or before her illnesses?

She had already been confined for mental illness.

I'd like to read that. Why wouldn't such a project be of interest to a Hollywood studio?

Awful . . . Hollywood! I would not work with them voluntarily. But we tried to get American money, outside a studio . . . *(Shrugs.)* Not interested. Most of them didn't know who she was.

Signor Visconti, I'm told that you are your own best public

relations man. That you use, or employ, the . . . élite to spread word of your pictures to . . . the public?

I have friends—people who have influence . . . and taste. They come to visit while I am making a picture, they see it in a screening, they go to the premiere, the film festivals, then they talk. . . . And so everybody else wants to *know*. It *is* very useful. In America, one cannot do this. It is a bigger country, and does not have so much of an élite class; *you* have television, instead.

I'd hate to think television takes the place of any kind of élite!

But Americans don't like an élite, *vero?*

Not a hereditary élite. But there's always an élite of some kind, isn't there?

Quality rises to the top, no?

We're taught that . . . Tell me something: Is there a casting couch in Italian cinema, as in Hollywood?

More. . . .

More sexist, too, I'd imagine.

Yes. To be a young, pretty female . . . *(Mock-shudders.)* But every kind of sex, on the couch.

Well, sex is sex. By the way, I haven't really touched on your family life.

Then you haven't been interested enough to ask.

Not at all, I just didn't want to intrude on your privacy.

It is all right. My family is a happy thing for me—so many of us, nobody is stuck together like glue. And each one is interesting, so I cannot be the speaker for anyone but for Luchino.

Is it because you have Germanic roots that you're so interested in German characters in your films, and in Mann?

I like the German personality—with the big exception of the Nazi madness. I feel almost German, sometimes. I am more calm than most of my country's people. Many of my friends are German. . . .

Or Austrian—like Herr Berger.

Yes . . . What would you like to know about Helmut?

Well, why does he play gigolos so often, or so well?

(Drily.) Ask him.

I didn't mean to imply anything. But his screen persona *isn't* likable. . . .

Ah! In America, you want every woman vulnerable, every actor "likable."

Women in Italian cinema aren't exactly impregnable. . . .

(Laughs; both laugh.) Vero, vero. As you know, Helmut is a good friend of mine, so I think we should talk about somebody else.

Well, about the *professional* relationship with Berger: you know, in America, such a continued . . . patronship would be rather harmful to most male directors. . . .

The fear of man-to-man relationships on every level . . . But I do not live or work in America. *(Smiles.)*

What do you think of Italian and other European directors who go to make an English-language film in America?

I understand this temptation. I know that the studio gives them everything on a silver tray, then forgets the name of the director when it is finished.

Because the film flops?

It *has* to . . . "flop." Because it is not American, yet it is not any other nationality.

A strange mutant . . . You understand the temptation, but you successfully resist it?

I have experience with the American money men. I think most American people are nice people, but the businessmen, they have no souls.

Let alone artistic insight? . . . Do you also find that Europe is more tolerant and nurturing of the great homosexual intellect?

Sì.

How so?

What do you want to know, about whom?

About your own work.

I do not want to give new information about *me*. What they know, they already know. Let them find out more from what I do, what I create—not what I say to a question. . . .

Was I trespassing on your privacy, Maestro?

(Offers hands, palms upward.) No . . . You have strong curiosity, it is good. But you will learn that it is not always practical. Sometimes, the back of the hand comes down to stop it. But not now . . . You are interested in movies?

Who isn't?

You are from California.

Yes. *(Both laugh.)* But not necessarily sentenced to it.

Then you like New York?

New York, Europe, the world . . . The world *is* your oyster, isn't it, Signor Visconti?

No. *(Shakes head, smiling.)* Not now. Not in a wheelchair. But soon. When this picture is completed, I will watch it. And like everyone else, I will forget there is a wheelchair.

Cecil Beaton

1904–1980

I MET Cecil Beaton in June 1970, at a party in London. The party was memorable to a sixteen-year-old chiefly for two reasons. The first was Cathleen Nesbitt, then in her early eighties but seemingly much younger and sprier. I didn't know she was a good friend of Beaton's. To me, she was the actress who'd played Hayley Mills's Boston grandmother in a favorite film, *The Parent Trap*. I had no way of knowing that her most famous role was as Rex Harrison's mother in the stage production of *My Fair Lady*.

The other reason the evening stood out was all the talk about E. M. Forster, who had just died at the age of ninety-one. To a teenager, Forster was one on a list of musty, must-read authors. An American English teacher had recommended that I read *Howard's End*, a less than inviting title. The recommendation was not taken up for many years, until the novel was vaguely but temptingly referred to and described in the movie *Educating Rita*.

Meeting Mr. Beaton—not yet a Sir—was, frankly, unmemorable, though it was at the behest of my grandfather, General Ruben Garcia. A friend of Beaton's, Granddad had served in Mexico's diplomatic service in Britain, France, and Chile, and lived in London with my mother and one of my aunts for two years just after World War II. It was strange to discuss my grandfather, an ardent Mexican patriot and author, with this consummately English gent whose flat-crowned hat and apricot ascot lent a bohemian air to the Mayfair townhouse. He asked me to call him Cecil, which I hesitated to do, especially since the invitation was less than heartfelt; it was a lesser evil than calling him Mr. Beaton, an appellation which precluded familiarity. Cecil's mercurial eyes indicated that

56

he'd rather surrender some dignity—lost, anyway, on an American teenager—than the possibility of fun, even romance.

But almost anything connected with my grandfather inspired in me a certain respectfulness. Beaton and I had two brief conversations that evening, bridged by an interlude with a young woman who'd seen *The Parent Trap* and had no desire to discuss Forster. So the problem of appellation didn't arise that night. Mostly, Beaton spoke and I half-listened. I lent an incredulous ear when he informed me that my grandfather's moviegoing passion was Greta Garbo, whom Beaton knew *very* well—I'd only seen her in *Grand Hotel*. Vainly, he'd tried to persuade Garbo to meet Granddad in 1946, he said. I could scarcely believe my ears. *Abuelito* had always told me his favorite movie stars were the Mexican actress Maria Felix and, despite her being a Spaniard, Sarita Montiel, who for a while adopted Mexico after abandoning Hollywood, Burt Lancaster, and Gary Cooper (her costars in *Vera Cruz*).

In England for the first time in four long years, I wanted to see more of the countryside. Cecil kindly obliged, telling me how to reach his home, Reddish House, Broadchalke, by rail . . . His car met me at the station, and from his headquarters we explored the Salisbury Plain and other aspects of Wiltshire, over the long weekend.

As I learned about the many books he'd published, starting with *Beaton's Book of Beauty* in 1930, my interest grew. I confided my own journalistic aspirations, and the more Cecil told me of his life and times, his work photographing and meeting "*every*body," the more I wanted someday to interview him. The man's work definitely overshadowed the man. It seemed never-ending. His leisure, he pointed out, was "precious and rare," and by the end of my stay, I felt I'd been privileged to get to know and spend time with this elegant, sometimes warm, sometimes frosty dynamo.

After the movie *My Fair Lady*, which earned him his second and third Oscars, Beaton—once called "that transmogrified Yellow Book soul"—swung into the sixties. He met, photographed, and befriended the likes of Mick Jagger and Rudolf Nureyev. He designed, he lived, and he "chronicled" in the series of diaries he'd begun in the early twenties. More books came out. And Cecil almost did—at least, he was less cautious about hiding his sexuality than in decades past. Almost to the end, he remained sexually and professionally active. (Ex-pal Truman Capote had Beaton say in

Answered Prayers, "The most distressing fact of growing older is that I find my private parts are shrinking.") But the work, and its consistency, came first. In 1979, the year of our interviews, he told me the two reasons he'd so admired Forster: one, he outlived most of his contemporaries, including his critics; and two, though surprisingly unprolific, Forster had written novels whose worth endured from one era to another.

Isn't it ironic that George Cukor never won an Academy Award until *My Fair Lady*, by which time you'd won one for *Gigi*, for costume design, and that you won *two*, for costume and set designs, for *MFL*?

(Smiles graciously.)

Rumor of your feud with Cukor has been rampant ever since *MFL*.

We hit it off immediately. We admired each other's talents, and I thought he would be the right director for *My Fair Lady*—not that it was my choice. Jack Warner was very much in charge, but wise enough to leave the artistic decisions to us.

Once the casting ones were made—he'd wanted Cary Grant for Henry Higgins!

He put financial considerations first.

What specific incident happened to alienate you and Cukor?

I will name *one* . . . I took several photographs of Miss Hepburn, in her own and other players' costumes. Cukor thought it wasn't the time or place, which it was. He didn't want his star tired, and she wasn't. Whether he saw it as a usurpation of his authority was never clear to me. He was angry, and won the show of strength; Miss Hepburn had to defer to her director. But I had the photographs.

Which were published in a beautiful volume on the film.

Yes, and well worth it. Miss Hepburn was an ideal subject. I coaxed the heavy eye makeup off her, and we developed what she called her Flemish look. Interesting, because she was born in Belgium, you know.

When you did *MFL*, did you realize it would be the highlight of your designing career?

I knew I was at my creative peak. I was able to draw upon my by then vast knowledge of history and detail, photography, design, and so on. When it came time to do the motion picture, I was disappointed it was not shot in London. However, I had plenty of time to get over it, and my stay in California was for the most part pleasant.

What was the name of the gay bar you frequented in Los Angeles, at the time?

I don't remember. Brain fag, you know.

Was collaborating with Vincente Minnelli, on *Gigi*, easier?

Minnelli is a more easygoing chap. Less dictatorial.

You also worked with Minnelli in *On a Clear Day You Can See Forever*. To the best of my knowledge, Minnelli is heterosexual, though one of Judy Garland's biographers wrote that she suspected him of having an affair with Gene Kelly while she was married to him. Isn't it ironic, or sad anyway, that two gay men didn't get along as well as a gay man and a straight one?

I don't know. (*Shrugs.*) Personalities. On the other hand, the unapproved-of are often . . . almost goaded into competition. Look what happens when women work together. Very often, they're expected to fight, on some level. For the amusement of the men working with them. I don't know if this happens with blacks. It happens with homosexuals, sometimes, with Jews, frequently. Perhaps my will was stronger by the time I worked with Mr. Cukor.

Some people said that you felt *MFL* was *yours*.

It is, in a way. But I was not directing . . .

I'll bet you wanted to direct, Sir—more than once?

Yes. It's easy to wish to. Difficult to carry out. I had, have, a strong will. But directing people to carry it out is another matter. Quite entirely another matter.

You have acted. Why didn't you pursue acting as another career?

I suffered from stage fright, and I didn't project a strong enough personality for the stage. I also didn't have the time, once I was working at different things. I never had the organization to juggle too many things at once, and I liked to be able to concentrate on the project at hand.

Do you like actors and actresses?

I find most actors insufferably egotistical. However, some actresses are decorative and pleasantly egotistical.

Is your friend Cathleen Nesbitt egotistical? She never gives that impression.

Ever. She's not. Very dear lady. But like many in her profession, her choices are sometimes dismaying. Did you see her in that abomination, *Staircase?*

When it came out, I was too young to be allowed to see it, in America. Then it disappeared forever.

A homosexual love-hate story. Terribly depressing and unreal, in fact. Cathleen played the invalid mother who lived upstairs— Burton's mother [the film costarred Richard Burton and Rex Harrison]. Utter, ugly realism, I suppose they call it. It was degrading, the way they'd got her up. Where is the woman's dignity, which she has irredeemably earned over the years? Disgusting! Poor Cathleen.

Speaking of *Staircase,* it's well known that Rex Harrison is very homophobic. What do you think of that?

It's a shame, of course. I've heard he never liked Noel.

Which is bizarre, when you consider that Harrison's biggest movie hit before *MFL* was Noel Coward's *Blithe Spirit.* And he finally won his Oscar, for *MFL,* under a gay man's direction.

That's true. Well, I hadn't looked at it that way.

You had an on-again-off-again relationship with Noel Coward. . . .

When we first met, I admired him enormously. And I envied his flair. He was so at ease with strangers. That took me many, many years to effect. But he didn't seem to take notice of me— and I'd so wanted to make an impression.

What was his sartorial advice to you, when you met?

Well, on shipboard, he tried to advise me. I recall it precisely.
He said, "A polo jumper or unfortunate tie exposes one to danger."
He was very well-meaning.

Why didn't you become close friends?

Who can say? Perhaps a clash of personalities. But we did enjoy
each other's company. Though I *told* Noel when he began to gain
all the weight, and he took it personally. It was meant esthetically;
he worshipped beauty, and don't we all.

**Let's go back. Way back, to your school days. You attended
Harrow . . .**

Harrow, yes. It seems so long past. I'll always remember that
in school—earlier—I made excellent bait for the bully boys.

Did you feel *different* from the beginning?

Special, in a way. So you could describe that as different.

Was your younger brother Reggie your friend?

We had different interests—different worlds, really.

**Excuse me for saying so, Sir, but you sometimes give the
impression of bloodlessness. Your whole life, you've been thin.
But *you* proved the strong one, didn't you?**

That is true. I resisted bully boys, and I've resisted adversity
ever since, with every ounce of resistance.

**How did Reggie's untimely death affect you? [Reggie Beaton
died beneath the wheels of a train, in 1933.]**

I missed him . . . after he was gone. None of us could believe
it. The worst thing was the inquest, the hearing. The verdict . . .
that it was a suicide, because of Reggie's health. My mother never
got over that. I never could believe he chose to end his life.

**I read in one of your published diaries that you felt *you* should
have died, instead. Why?**

It was a feeling, at the time. Reggie was so vital and alive, so
well-liked. I felt guilty that we hadn't shared more. As the elder

brother, I should have taken the initiative. I was too often disdainful toward him.

You've also written that he was your parents' favorite.

He was. . . . I virtually believed his death would end Mum's life. My father, though, died long before she did.

Do you think Reggie was their favorite because he was hetero-sexual?

It played its part. Reggie was also less ambitious than I.

Do you think gayness engenders extraordinary ambition?

I don't know. I think it might do, in those who are ambitious to begin with. Work can become a proving ground. . . .

Where sex might be the proving ground for the heterosexual male? What was your relationship with your father like?

It wasn't part of the Freudian pattern; we got on splendidly, in general. He was very self-effacing, a kind man. I loved him. We were as close as a father and son would be, in those days. I never felt starved of his affection, though again, after he had left us, I felt sorry I hadn't spent more time with him, spoken with him more.

You were closer to your sisters?

Yes. Logically, because Reggie was out in cars, then out chasing girls in cars. And unlike Reggie, Baba and Nancy were very willing photographic subjects. They were my first models, though I sometimes used my mother. Of course, women were considered more apt and more appropriate as subjects for the camera.

In the early 1920s you did several portraits of yourself and your fellow students, in female drag and dandyesque costumes. Were most of your subjects gay young men?

Gay young men! Indeed they were, in a sense. (*Laughs.*) But . . . *then*, it was never said aloud. Now it's so casual. "Bent" was a more common term. We used the word "gay" so much; heterosexuals—another recently reactivated word—did also.

Did you enjoy wearing costumes?

I didn't enjoy posing. One never likes one's looks. But I wanted photos of myself for . . . eternity—another youthful, silly word.

Was most of your set homosexual?

One never knew for sure! Even if there was sex, most of us believed it was a passing . . .

Just a passing fanny?

Precisely. Romantic love was in books, always between a strong male and a weak female. Most everyone married and had families, regardless. As in Japan today, where marriage is a requirement of adulthood, but is at least offset by no moral censure against homosexual affairs.

Did you think you would contractually marry?

I believed I might. Most of us didn't have pleasant feelings about the future, except financially. Most of my friends had money, or their families did. I don't remember any male who looked forward to being married or a father. We all wanted to avoid becoming like our own models at home.

Were they happy times, in school?

Generally. I did have one deep regret: my blond friend Dadie Rylands, who later worked at the Woolfs' Hogarth Press, was at King's; I was at St. John's [Cambridge] . . .

Were they very sexual times?

There *was* lovemaking. But nothing was blatant. Today it's all sex, no romance. All blatant and untextured.

And yet, in the twenties, homosexuality was a totally taboo subject. It's still taboo, but nowhere to the same degree. . . .

Homosexuality is more acceptable, only because blatant heterosexuality is more acceptable.

Did your parents approve of your artistic aspirations?

My father put me to work—*business*. I finally quit in . . . 1926. Only then did I learn that the one pound weekly which I'd been earning had been paid by my father. He knew I'd never be a businessman, but he wanted me to experience discipline. He was kind, really.

After your sisters, your earliest subjects included the fascinating Sitwells.

Edith was a born *poseuse*. Her gay brother Osbert rather liked it too. Edith was one of the few unattractive women who relished posing. The Sitwells were very useful, for they knew so many people. Being British, they helped me. By contrast, Diaghilev was very selfish of his contacts. He knew that his approval was enough of a spur to a young artist.

You met him in Venice. What was he like?

Not attractive, only magnificent. Rather stout. But you see, in those days, someone like me was unattractively thin. Thin . . . was not "in." Diaghilev was kind enough to review my portfolio. He seemed distracted and not very interested. Until he saw my photographs of Nancy and Baba. He wasn't impressed by my sketches, but he did like my photographs. Although he didn't choose me to do set designs, I felt elated by his interest in *some* aspect of my work. It made me more hopeful.

After all, your photography was your main . . . line. Why did you choose to become a photographer?

I like to feel that photography chose me. Cameras were not taken for granted then. They were miraculous, although I was born long after they came into being. Something I realized quite early was that a photographer, in searching for special and attractive settings, got to go where ordinary people didn't. As a child, I reviewed several photographs by other photographers, of beautiful *rooms*. The kind of places I wanted to go to, and inhabit. I wanted to have a life lived in beautiful rooms.

Wasn't there also an element of controlling the situation, as a photographer, someone who arranges and poses others?

That was an attraction, as well. Being rather shy—well, painfully shy, to be more exact—I could use the camera as a go-between. I was very good—socially and professionally—if I had a camera in the same room with me.

It was your element. Did you enjoy your personal life then?

As an artist, I wasn't divided into an office life and an at-home life. So it was more complex, more rewarding, than the average. And what price there was to pay, I did so.

What price did you pay, Sir?

I'm speaking metaphorically, and . . . personally.

Was the transition from Cambridge to working life traumatic, or were the upper classes sheltered even in the real world?

It was definitely not traumatic. I think that regardless of class, after the Great War, people were anything but innocent or dewy-eyed. We weren't sheltered; the Victorian age had become an ancient world by then. . . . One thing I gather is that nowadays, students—including the females—are more devoted to their studies. We were there because it was what one did. It had less to do with a degree . . . It was the last golden time before having to work or assume adult responsibilities. So we played—how we played! And we knew we were special. Especially those who had money. I was almost as cocky—I knew I had talent.

In your early career, much time was spent photographing society matrons. Didn't pendulous chins and bosoms become something of a bore?

I had very few of those. Most of the society *crème de la crème* were young things who wanted immortality *before* they became pendulous.

Did you actively seek to become a celebrity yourself?

I gained publicity, which was easier to do then. So I became *known*. This word *famous*, it wasn't as common, nor as vulgar, as today. What I wanted was twofold: enough money to live very well, and to be an Artiste, capital A.

Sir, would you call yourself an esthete?

Of course! From the earliest age. We weren't rich, but I aspired to these other, beautiful rooms. I felt that life must be more special, more . . . supernal, in such rooms. How they could gild your soul and senses! You can easily become your environment. . . .

Before *My Fair Lady,* you were best known as a photographer, primarily of the rich and fashionable. You've been painted by Tchelitchew, among others, but perhaps the definitive Beaton portrait is one that you yourself took, in which your suit is covered with your photographs, and the photographs seem to become your clothes. And they do say that clothes make the man, Sir Cecil. . . .

(Smiles broadly.) And your question is?

Well, the portrait made me wonder, what lies beneath the well-known photographer-designer?

Well, perhaps not a glittering personality. It's a two-edged question. I can't answer without seeming pompous or maudlin. I may answer it incorrectly.

But compared to, say, Coward, you're very private. Are you content to let your work speak entirely for you?

Coward and the rest were a different type. They spoke as much as their work did. Photographers—and this *is* my basic calling and my calling card—are far more reticent. Then *or* now. I suppose because we record, or chronicle. We're more interested in viewing and capturing life's stage, than in taking up the stage and ignoring the other players.

Do other people interest you, even yet?

Somebody probably notorious once said that when he wasn't thinking or speaking of himself, he wasn't thinking or speaking. Yes, people do fascinate, don't they?

Through his shutter, Beaton met the rich and famous. In the 1920s he was a protégé of the colorful Baron de Meyer. The German photographer was married to the equally gay Olga Carracciolo, a probable daughter of Edward VII. The gay couple was socially prominent, and the baron introduced Beaton to many crucial contacts. In 1930, accompanied by Anita Loos and her husband, Cecil finally made it to Hollywood, where he was given carte blanche to photograph the top stars. His prize quarry, however, eluded him. Garbo would not cooperate; Beaton didn't make her acquaintance until 1932. It was a relationship which would, on and off, endure through several years, even taking the unlikely turn of a marriage proposal. More than John Gilbert or any other man, Beaton came closest to wedding the divine Garbo. Even after Garbo went her separate, irrevocable way—precipitated by publication of various photos by Beaton in *Vogue* and extensive press coverage in the late forties of their "affair"—Beaton maintained that Garbo was the most beautiful of all his subjects. It was quite a tribute from a man whose collection of negatives numbered a well-catalogued 250,000.

What about the much-written-about Garbo-Gilbert affair?

Definitely overrated. It was with Dietrich that Gilbert had a passionate affair. But both were married, so it was impossible. When Garbo did speak of Gilbert, it was as though she were discussing a *brother*. The story of his high-pitched voice ruining his career was also inaccurate.

Then how did he lose his career?

It's been told in detail elsewhere; he crossed one of the Higher Powers. I don't recall if it was an M, a G, or an M.

More careers than we suspect probably ended that way. But back to Garbo. Did you think you'd never get to meet her, after your 1930–31 stay in Hollywood?

I despaired. . . .

You met at the house of Edmund Goulding and his wife. . . .

Let me interrupt you. Edmund was a leading director. Homosexual. English. Delightful. The meeting wasn't arranged, but the Gouldings were friends with Garbo, and I was staying at their home. She *arrived* one night. I didn't wish—after I heard her unmistakable voice and nearly panicked, I didn't have *any* desire—to intrude upon her privacy. But I was called downstairs, we met, and we became old friends almost immediately. It was perhaps the most unforgettable evening of my life.

A meeting with the unicorn.

Yes. A white unicorn. She was dressed in white, very tanned. It's in one of my books.

Emotionally, what was she like then, at the height of her fame?

Moody—when a mood would take her, she gave in to it totally. She would hole up for days at a time in her bungalow, or take off for a nature-haven hideaway, playing the role of nymph. She lived in nature. When I finally met her, some of the mystery vanished. She was very down-to-earth, hated profanity and indignities like a man patting a woman on the derrière. But she was fascinating. Maddening, as well—very egocentric.

But apparently it was an ego that people were willing to cater to?

Yes, because she was *real* . . . never pretentious. She was egocentric in a limited way.

Were you romantically attracted to her?

(A pause.) Yes.

Was she the first woman you were romantically attracted to?

She was the only one I wanted to marry. Later on, that is. Once I'd attained my own degree of success. It would have been an achievement. It was an achievement to keep in touch with her.

Why did she decline to marry?

She could never be married. She insisted that it would place her inside a cage. The thought of it alarmed her and quite altered our relationship.

Would it have been, as they say, a marriage of convenience?

I don't know if it would have been convenient or not. I never found out.

Your 1946 photos of Garbo are the best testament to the splendor of her middle age. How did those come about?

Thank you. But . . . *if* one is interested in my work, I presuppose a willingness to read about it. I know *you* have read, but it's no good someone just reading an interview with Cecil Beaton and expecting it all to fit in there. A life doesn't fit into an interview, I want to make that clear, in case you have any younger readers.

An interview with an interesting personality often leads to further reading, though.

Well, in my view, the interview should be the dessert, after the main courses of reading and research.

Young people seem to read less now, but the interview format is as strong as ever, don't you think?

I keep up on youth; they can keep up on me. Now, to get back to what you asked, Garbo sometimes lost her inhibitions and blossomed. When she was most herself, I asked to take some pictures. She agreed, and it was assumed that *one* would appear in *Vogue*. That's not quite how it turned out, through no fault of my own.

Did that end or sour your relationship?

Not really. Or not to my knowledge. Garbo was realistic about publicity. But speculation about marriage, even in the press, alarmed her.

You and Tennessee Williams wanted Garbo to play Blanche in *Streetcar*.

It's a myth about Garbo—she never decided to retire, until perhaps in the last ten years. Now her legend allows her no choice. Tennessee and I might have collaborated, but when Garbo read *Streetcar*, she didn't feel anything for the Blanche character. Garbo is not script-wise. She felt Blanche was too feminine and self-deceiving. She also hated that she lied so much.

But lying is Blanche's survival mechanism!

Garbo felt she was a fool.

A most un-Scandinavian character, I suppose. Poor Blanche . . . Was Garbo still hoping to find the right script, in those days?

She didn't search for the *script*. She had characters she wanted to play. Most especially Elizabeth of Austria. She almost played the role in *The Eagle with Two Heads*. [Tallulah Bankhead eventually did it.]

Did the premarital publicity about you and Garbo give you pleasure or satisfaction?

Of course.

But any man who would have married her would have ended up as Mr. Garbo.

(Hesitates.) Possibly.

Of course, it would have been a stunning triumph.

Without a question. . . .

When you were at Cambridge, for instance, did you believe you would marry?

It was vaguely assumed. In between the usual protestations of youth.

Other than Garbo, did you ever come close to, or propose, contractual marriage?

When you say *contractual* . . .

I mean a heterosexual marriage-through-the-state. There are heterosexual and homosexual marriages, unions, which don't have the benefit of a contract.

It *is* very revealing that a marriage contract, now you mention it, is the only agreement between two people which cannot be terminated by the pair's mutual consent.

The state must consent, as well. So did you come close to marriage with a woman?

Well, if one can't have Garbo . . .

Have you regretted, for whatever reason, not marrying?

No.

Do you think most of the public is aware that you're gay?

I'm not sure what the public generally is aware of. I think if they are aware of non-pop personalities, they dwell upon a heterosexual image, be it real or manufactured.

Would you ever—like a David Bowie or other star—make a public announcement of your sexuality?

What nonsense! Why should anyone do such a thing?

Would you rather have grown up in today's more sexually free climate?

In any age, talent and social position make freedom easier. But growing up wasn't as . . . blatantly sexual, or violent, as it appears to be nowadays. I can't see an advantage in growing up today. Before the Great War—the First World War—it was more . . . nostalgic and genteel. I remember my childhood with enormous affection. It was a wonderful time. I wouldn't know where to begin, today. . . .

How, if at all, have homosexuals changed?

In visibility and daring. But there are still grave limits, affection between men being even more risky than sex.

You mean in public?

Of course.

How do you feel about drag queens and feminine men?

Many of the latter are heterosexual, although the effeminate man is an old stereotype. *I* don't feel masculinity need be forced, and extreme masculinity is something of a charade—it has a rather ludicrous quality. But a truly feminine man, like a truly masculine woman, will never do. It doesn't fit, and it's self-destructing. If the majority of heterosexuals persist in believing the stereotype, it's their misfortune; it can prevent them from honest, gratifying re-lationships.

How important has sex been in your life, Sir?

Well, young man . . . I think it assumed its proper place, which is somewhere in the middle.

Which was your ruling passion: sex or work?

Was? (Smiles indulgently.) Let's see . . . Only a thriving courtesan could honestly say *both.* Sex was no less enjoyable, but it was less. It took less time, less thought, and though intense and passionate, sex was never a ruling *design* of one's life. Overall, it wasn't as significant.

Your private life has been very private. But were there great love relationships?

Let me tell you something that Mae West said. She was asked

about the men she was seen with in public. And she replied, "It's not the men you see me with, it's the men you don't see me with. . . ." That is true of everybody in public life.

And no doubt more true of gay people in public life, appearing with the opposite sex, but living the real life behind closed doors.

(Shrugs.) No choice. Now, you asked about my relationships. Well, no life can pass, eventfully, without one or two—what did you call them?

Great love relationships.

And I had my share. No regrets in that sphere.

But you've been a loner. . . .

By choice. Without regrets.

Beaton was a self-confessed snob. But he was quick to point out that he wasn't a snob of "the first water." Such a snob was Beaton's houseguest Evelyn Waugh, whom he couldn't abide. Considering their time and place, it shouldn't be a surprise that gay men like Beaton or Coward could be somewhat homophobic. Coward once said that a trio of gay men was a "crowd," and Beaton admitted, "I feel less conspicuous in the company of women of intelligence." Both men endorsed the status quo and its attendant imperialism —Coward detested Gandhi. And like many or most of his class, Cecil Beaton was given to racism and anti-Semitism.

In 1938 he illustrated a *Vogue* article about show-biz folk invading Long Island high society. The piece itself wasn't anti-Semitic—in contrast to Beaton's florid illustration, which garlanded such names as Goldwyn, Mayer, and Selznick, and tossed in two "kike"s for ill measure. An uproar ensued, the issue was reprinted, and there was talk of Condé Nast's magazine going under, once advertisers began to secede. Beaton's contract was terminated; he later went to work for *Harper's Bazaar*, but continued to do assignments for *Vogue* in subsequent decades.

Before the first interview at Reddish House was arranged, I let Beaton know that I was part Jewish on my father's side. And that I'd spent the previous summer in Israel. During the interview, he made no inquiry into my ancestry, but asked about the scenery in Israel, particularly Jaffa, of orange fame. I also confessed that I was a Barbra Streisand fan. Sir Cecil's last major movie assignment had been Streisand's third film, *On a Clear Day You Can See Forever*. He designed the costumes for the lush reincarnation sequences, which were shot inside the Royal Pavilion at Brighton, a moviemaking first.

Despite, and even perhaps because of, the picture's lack of financial success, Beaton relished discussing it—among his best film work—and his collaboration with Streisand. Afterward, I was surprised by how much we had said about the singer-actress. As fate would have it, the Streisand material was the first to see print, once specialized periodicals on the star began to proliferate. In the years closely preceding and following his death, Beaton elicited scant interest from magazine editors. The expert on the Edwardian, Regency, and other periods was deemed antiquarian, irrelevant to the spiritual seventies or the aching eighties.

I first heard of the anti-Semitic "joke" while working at Condé Nast in 1975. The information dampened my desire to interview Sir Cecil. But after I read that a stroke had paralyzed his right arm, I sent him a note of condolence, and waited. With the steeliness that characterized him, Sir Cecil gradually taught himself to be left-handed. He began by signing his name, then writing letters, sketching, painting in watercolors and oil, and resuming photography—with a tripod. However, he didn't keep up his historic diaries.

Sir, there are still rumors of your anti-Semitism. . . .

Well, I believe I've pleaded guilty to that once or twice. I don't think anyone is spotless.

Do you suppose the rumors pretty much all stem from the *Vogue* incident?

I hope so. And that was very long ago.

I'm always confounded when a member of one minority looks down on another minority. Why do you think that is?

What, that you're bloody confounded, or why one looks down on another? I don't know. What a boring topic . . . At Harrow and elsewhere, we were taught that we would inherit the earth . . . from our fathers. We were the masters.

Meaning white heterosexual Christian Protestant males. . . .

Of course. They teach and cherish prejudice. As times have changed, my mind has too. But I'm not about to apologize for my past here. It's far too late for that.

You're not anti-Semitic today?

No.

Do you believe Christianity is the "true" religion?

I never believed that. Except superficially; one follows the *forms*, in society. Those who didn't like Jews weren't usually religious fanatics. They were social leaders.

Well, none of it makes sense. Let's move on to Gertrude Stein. What did you think of her?

I visited her Paris apartment in 1935. The impression I got was that she genuinely liked some men but was never unguardedly natural in their presence. I was fascinated by her well-ordered ugliness—she, her companion, the apartment, were all calculatedly, spotlessly plain. Not in an unattractive way, however. For the details, you'll have to read the appropriate book. Miss Stein was a contrast to almost every woman I ever photographed.

I imagine she didn't like strong personalities. She did think less of photographers than of painters. To her mind, there was less creativity involved. And as a masculine personality, she had little patience with traditional femininity in general.

Stein preferred macho males like Hemingway or Picasso?

Yes. But their strength, their personalities, were sublimated into their work. They in no way threatened her, as a strong heterosexual who was not an artist might have. She didn't . . . for example, Miss Stein would not have approved of a strong personality like Quentin Crisp—to give you an idea of what I term strength.

That seems strange, because Mr. Crisp, though a survivor, makes no attempt to hide his natural femininity.

His strength, though, is his exterior self, not his work. The unchangeability. As you say, a survivor. This may be why he achieved some measure of fame late in life. Strong work is less threatening to most people than strong personalities. And at that time, many of the stronger personalities were nonheterosexual.

In the arts?

In all the arts. Extraordinary people lived and worked then.

Were you strong or authoritative, besides being a survivor?

I was strong through my work, but somewhat repressed outside the company of my family. On the stage, I could never play myself. That self was not commercially transferable. You would have found that some of the strongest male screen personalities in Hollywood were strong through their *work*—on the screen, only.

I'm assuming you're referring to early-thirties Hollywood. Were you aware of homosexual activity there, at the time and beyond?

One could hardly fail to be. From the inside, everybody knows what the rest of the nation doesn't even suspect. . . .

Did you have any affairs in Hollywood?

I wouldn't name-drop. Gossip is far more pleasant than name-dropping, for it concerns others.

This sounds like a latter-day Oscar Wilde! What influence, if any, did Wilde have on you or on others of your set, while you were growing up?

A very negative influence, indeed, in terms of being honest about one's difference. The *name* was not spoken, and from time to time there were tidbits of news meant to intimidate anyone who might follow in his footsteps. The shame of his poor family was dwelt upon—how they had had to change their name, been denied lodgings while traveling, and so forth.

Did you know his son, Vyvyan Holland?

Yes, quite well. He always—no, that is imprecise; he seldom spoke of his father, but when he did, it was very affectionately. He was a good father and, perhaps understandably, not as good a husband.

Have you known many homosexual or bisexual fathers?

Not carnally, if that's what you're seeking.

Sir Cecil! Really. You know what I mean. How would you, from your perspective, rate such fathers?

On the whole, I think they are more doting fathers. And I do *not* believe that doting upon a child spoils him for life.

Holland was married. But was he heterosexual? I know he had many gay friends.

In the case of Oscar Wilde's son, if you don't already know the answer, it isn't for me to supply it. I remember that Thelma, Vyvyan's wife, was quite a *gourmande*. And she told me that "the father" had been taboo as a subject of discussion; his name wasn't even mentioned in the house, for many years.

Well, that's a twist. He's affectionately remembered, but he's a relation that dare not speak its name. . . . Let's get back to Gertrude Stein.

Back to back to back. *(Laughs shyly.)*

Yes, yes, yes. You re-met Gertrude ten years later? I remember a portrait you did of her: two exposures in one setting.

Yes. That was a decade later, and age had not withered her ugliness.

I take it you didn't fawn over her?

She rather ignored me. Even giving me the grand tour of that apartment—her new one, on the Rue Christine—it could have been anyone on that *tourette*. Miss Toklas, I recall, stayed in her room sewing. *She* seemed nice, but was little more than a servant.

Much more than that, one would think. Didn't you get a sense of the lasting love between the two women?

One used the other, the other allowed herself to . . . *most* famous couples are like that. Except that each usually uses the other; few people I've met were as passive as Miss Toklas. Olivier and Vivien Leigh—each used the other, and they reveled in it. The same with Burton and Taylor, and others.

Moving on to another strong personality: Ms. Streisand.

Ah, yes, dear Miss Streisand.

You got along pretty well, didn't you?

Quite well.

How do you account for that, when there are so many stories about her and her coworkers not getting along?

Hmmm. Well, she's a woman with power. I'm used to that sort. I *like* that sort—thinking, working women. Also, you have to take anything dramatic which you read with a grain of salt. A pillar of salt, perhaps. People are only people; newspapers create the drama, which makes life more interesting.

But you and Cukor . . .

Even that has been exaggerated. Most of the time, we *did* get along. We simply had an incident or two . . . some competition. We *knew* the other's game. But there were no stormings off the set, no bitter feud. I rather hate to overemphasize this—it sounds so bland. Just say we didn't get along. . . .

Well, what was Streisand like, then?

Hmmm. Barbra is one of two kinds of, as you would now say, superstars. The two types are: the coolly detached and the fanatically involved. Barbra was the latter. The former type is typified by Audrey Hepburn. Both women are very different, yet they're both regal; that came through in the clothes I designed for them. Audrey cared about quality, too, but wasn't mesmerized by movies. Barbra and I talked our way into everything. I trusted her judgment, something I seldom do with any actor, especially a relative neophyte. She thought everything out; to this day, I've never met anyone so young who had such an awareness and knowledge of herself.

Did you like the finished product—the picture itself?

I recall that one of the reviewers found Streisand's performance as an English aristocrat reminiscent of vintage Joan Greenwood. I enjoyed reading that, because both women display a quality of cunning refinement. Barbra did an English accent to perfection . . . It is a pity she doesn't do more period material. She is an ideal mannequin and compelling in elegant costumes. Her face is a painting from several historical eras. Barbra as an Englishwoman, an Egyptian, or a Ming empress would be unforgettable.

The public sees her as very contemporary, but I think her essence is old-fashioned. In all honesty, she was far more likable, more at ease, in the old English sequences than as the neurotic college student in those dreadful miniskirt creations!

Didn't you ever quarrel?

We didn't. Both our reputations were on the line. She had done two previous musicals; this one had to be different. I had done musicals like *Gigi* and *My Fair Lady*, so how could I top myself? We topped ourselves visually. . . .

Many Streisand fans feel that her peak moment in movies is the Pavilion banquet scene where she's wearing a beehive bejeweled turban and flirting erotically—to the accompaniment of her own song—with John Richardson, a stunning blond.

Yes. That was very satisfying to see. . . . She was totally feminine, beguiling, shamelessly sexual—in the scene.

Did you two become close or at all intimate?

We were not terribly close, and I didn't want a closeness that would alter my feeling of her as a self-willed creation. Pleasing her was very difficult, but it pleased me, because *I* am extremely hard to please. Each of us is aware of the name we've been given and, more importantly, what we've each done with it.

In your work, have you found that you maybe get along better with, say, gay men or with straight men, or with strong women?

It depends. But sometimes, in getting closer to somebody, you find you have things in common. You get beneath the surface. But—as with, to some degree, Mr. Cukor—you find that those common traits or interests can divide you. I'd rather have a good working relationship with someone, than be a friend for a while and less than friendly thereafter.

In other words, high fences make good working relationships?

In a nutshell. I find that in work, intimacy can be a first step toward a lack of respect or, rather, a slovenly kind of familiarity. And with most superstars—which sounds silly if you say it fast—

I'd rather admire them on their pedestals than learn and experience all the disappointing details.

You took some of the best shots ever taken of Streisand. How do you rate her as a photographic subject?

She reminded me of Edith Sitwell. Truly, there is nothing new under the sun, and all people are basically variations of each other . . .

Now *I'll* interrupt: *Saroyan*.

I beg your pardon?

Saroyan: *The Time of Your Life*.

Oh . . . Sitwell and Streisand—both were very willing to experiment, even willing to compromise. Classically beautiful women are seldom willing to experiment. They are less evolved, because the mirror and the man tells them they've reached a state of perfection, never mind that it's subjective and entirely physical.

Yet you value the beautiful woman as a photographic subject, of course.

Yes . . . Isn't it appalling, the way a perfect camera subject like Elizabeth Taylor let herself become unphotographable. Barbra is a better photographic subject, though, because of her facial sculpture, the *planes*, and the chameleon quality she exudes.

Name some other great faces, ones the camera loved.

The classic face of all time, of course, belongs to Garbo. Not only because of the face, but due to her ability to paint it with moods, attitudes, emotions, suggestions. Dietrich's face was another camera dream, but more artifically so, more one-dimensional.

Does knowing somebody intimately make them a more or a less interesting subject? Does it detract from the mystery, or from the photographer's impartiality?

I have known Garbo intimately. Barbra was difficult to know— exasperating to know socially. Only the very complex or the very simple make marvelous subjects for photography or for costume design: a peasant in the Ukraine, a rice farmer in Burma, a Garbo, a Barbra Streisand. Not the housewife next-door, who might be simply complex to the point of stultification!

. . . I'll have to think that one out later.

Like Noel Coward, Beaton was a conservative gay man who was nonetheless long denied a knighthood by the queen. Yet he wouldn't utter a word against the royal family. One reason, perhaps: he was, for a time, the official Court photographer, in spite of his friendship with the Duke of Windsor, whom Queen Elizabeth—later the queen mother—resented.

When you were knighted, in 1972, how did you feel?

It was a painless process. But ten years too late for my mother to have enjoyed it. It made little difference, really, although it was, obviously, welcome.

Is the queen homophobic?

Officially, and on a subtle level, most public officials are supportive of the established order and way of doing things.

So why does the royal family have so many ardent gay supporters?

The royal household is the last vestige of elegance. The movies have certainly lost it. . . .

Were you close to the Duke of Windsor?

Nobody not of his station was close to him, emotionally, and he seemed a repressed man.

But nobody except his immediate family was "of his station."

Precisely. . . . But I did know him, and I met him often, to work with him. He very much admired my work, and he was pleasant enough. Of course, this grand passion he was supposed to have had for Wallis . . .

Do you mean it wasn't very evident?

He wasn't an emotional man.

It's been noted elsewhere that he may have been bisexual, and there is some legal evidence pertaining to a police raid . . .

I don't have that information.

So you wouldn't care to speculate or offer your own experiences as indications, one way or the other?

Not really. But do carry on.

All right. The Duchess of Windsor—was she pleasant?

She tried to behave nicely. He was devoted to her, and she ruled him.

Again, elsewhere it's been noted that she had a generous sexual appetite—without going into details. And that she had an affair, after marrying the ex-king, with the homosexual Woolworth heir.

That would be Jimmy Donohue . . . well, he was *also* married.

Digressing for a bit, but, Sir, *most* homosexual men or women, in those days, were contractually married. The very few exceptions include you and Gertrude Stein. How did you get away with it? Didn't being officially single shut a lot of doors to you?

Socially, I'm sure—well, I *know*—that it did. But being in the arts, and being extremely busy, I had a fair excuse. You know, the usual chitchat about "he hasn't found the right girl yet." My friendship with Garbo was a very good cover; one mentioned the *name* and people were mesmerized. Even though there was a period of ten years when we didn't see each other.

I see. . . . When the Duke and Duchess of Windsor were in exile . . .

Let's not talk about them. I don't think it's proper.

. . . Very well, sir. The present queen mother hired you as Court photographer, despite your friendship with her in-laws. Why?

She was sensible. She appreciated my work and knew I would photograph the royal family in a contemporary way, but with dignity.

You were close to Lord Mountbatten, and once posed on a sort of large bed with him, both of you lying down, looking up past the mirrors on the wall behind you.

What does that suggest to your fertile mind?

Comment, after the fact. I've always gotten the impression he

was a very nice man. And he *liked* the Mahatma Gandhi. Were
you and Mountbatten close—I mean, how close were you?

He was a very dear man. Carry on again.

You did a portrait of Princess Anne as a little blond tyke, on
Coronation Day, 1953. What are your impressions, as the royal
children have grown up?

Each is distinctly an individual. Anne perhaps most of all, being
the girl.

Do you know Prince Charles very well?

Yes. Very up-front.

Do you think he'll marry before he's forty? Or even thirty-five?

He'll have no choice, and he'll do what he's told.

What of the homosexual royals?

I cannot discuss what even I do not know.

You haven't even heard rumors? *I've* heard rumors. Or should
I carry on?

(Nods head, smiling.)

We'll move on to the show biz and political royalty whom you
got to meet and photograph; you know, it could have been you,
as well as Christopher Isherwood, who said, "I am a camera."

Ask, and I shall reveal. You've looked at many of the pictures.

Yes . . . Fred and Adele Astaire, in Condé Nast's apartment,
1930. I'm amazed that even then Fred's hairline went higher than
Everest. Did you sense his great dancing destiny?

Not *his!* His sister was the star of the family. Very sweet, so
talented. Of course, then came marriage. Fred was a nice enough
chap, as I recall. A bit cocky. Very American—you know, he had
so little, yet *so* confident. But as for film stardom, who could have
imagined it?

It might not have happened, without Ginger Rogers. Another
photo: a double-portrait of Auden, 1930, like Siamese twins.

Very snobbish. Smoked a lot. Those two things I remember.

Tell me, Sir, do snobs of a feather flock together?

(Both laugh.) Well, opposites rarely attract.

Uh-huh. Here: a 1931 piggyback, you carrying Anita Loos, in front of Hearst Castle.

She *was* saucy! It was funtime. The circus. Old Mr. Hearst and his circus of stars and flatterers. Still, the food was good, though I wasn't given enough time to relish it.

In 1931 you photographed MGM's finest, excepting you-know-who. Joan Crawford in an evening gown . . .

Desperate to get ahead.

Carry on, carry on. John Wayne.

So handsome. Very mild. *Very* mild. Originally named Marion Morrison.

It was said that his affair with Clara Bow began his career and ended hers.

In a sense; he was on a football team. Miss Bow supposedly got to know each member. The talk helped end her career in talkies, which wasn't as spectacular as her career in silents.

Proving, I guess, that silence is golden. . . . Tallulah and Marlene. Seems to me, personalities were stronger then.

Well . . . perhaps. *Women* seemed stronger; women like those two, when contrasted with the average demure female of the day.

Were you close to either Bankhead or Dietrich?

Tallulah was a friend, from London. She ruled the London stage as you young people have never seen anything ruled. But once talkies came in, she wanted so much to become a *true* star. Which, to her, meant moving pictures. She wanted to talk her way to posterity—she knew her voice could make the transition, and then some. But what Tallulah did was to make a horse's posterior of herself. She returned to the stage, and stayed. Dietrich was the best cameraman among Hollywood's actresses, before or since.

Rather dull—she loved housework, she kept saying—but spectacular-looking.

The shot of Johnny Weissmuller was daring by later standards, once censorship came in. Such a small loincloth . . .

Such a big talent . . . Oh, he seemed nice. He was still nice-looking in the face; by the 1940s, the body was still good but the face was coarse. He wasn't too intelligent. I was told that during World War II there was pressure for him to change his name. It was the studio—Jewish-owned and -run—which resisted. Anyway, by then he'd passed it.

Gary Cooper, also 1931.

Nothing like his stereotype of the slow-talking cowboy. Erudite, charming, spectacularly constructed man. Eddie [Goulding] once told me that he worshiped him—twice a day.

Were you a frequent worshiper?

Don't get me back into religious hot waters . . .

I believe it was Cooper's lover Lupe Velez who said that Cooper had the biggest organ in Hollywood, but no ass to push it with.

That's probably been said of half the actors in Hollywood.

And the other half?

Vice versa. . . .

Katharine Hepburn, 1934.

Loved to pose. That reminds me: she did a film about then, with Cukor, as a youth. The ads said—I remember distinctly—"She's a boy!" We had a lot of jokes among our set about that. . . .

You photographed her again, in the late 1960s, and she looked not only prettier, but more feminine. . . .

Not a bit of it! She *was* vulnerable, in front of the camera. Could shed a tear at the drop of a hat. But not someone easy to know. . . . I always wondered what she talked about in conversations, or if she had them.

In 1935 you took two leggy shots of Olivier and Gielgud. . . .

In *Romeo and Juliet*. One had the legs, the other the voice.

Did you have friendships with men in the theater?

Mostly with directors and producers. Actors are too flighty.

Salvador Dalí and his wife Gala. Did he ever strike you as gay, which is what one hears all the time?

No, he struck me as insane.

Interesting . . . We'll carry on, over into youth. You photographed Brando in a fawnlike pose in 1947. Was he fawnlike?

Lovely. Mumbly, even then. I hear he's gained weight. . . .

Plenty. Remember the John Huston film, from Carson McCullers, *Reflections in a Golden Eye*? It starred Taylor and Brando. I wonder how much they've gained between them?

I wouldn't want to wager. . . .

Who was the most . . . at-peace or happy individual you've photographed?

Well, the most serene was not Miss Kelly, but Krishnamurti, in the late 1950s. He had . . . a . . . *glow*. A holy man. Anyone who saw him could tell that. Not just his distinguished appearance. Rather, his ethereal . . . *(Pause.)* He *seemed* holy.

Does it anger or irritate you that your celebrity shots receive much more attention than your photos taken around the world during World War II, or pictures like *Bangkok Flour Factory*?

Please don't make my war tour sound like a pleasure cruise . . . *(Laughs.)* Yes. It bothers me. What can I do? Do you have a suggestion?

Afraid not . . . You did, for instance, homoerotic nudes of a black in Morocco, youths in Corsica, and you also did naked little children who were homeless after the war, in London. Was any of this criticized at the time?

Not the children, certainly. But the Corsican boys, in the late 1930s, were not everyone's cup of tea. *I* find nudes of girls in black stockings singularly unappetizing. But as long as one doesn't specialize in nudes, one won't be thought a pedestrian artist.

Or a gutter artist. Then, in the 1960s, you . . .

Allow me to interrupt. My career was not one continuous cycle of preening. I was let go by *Vogue*—a huge blow.

I didn't find any mention of *why*, in your diaries . . .

Obviously not. But decades do make a difference; eventually, one can admit to or say things. I can now reveal that many times, my work was considered outdated; shall I explain why? I captured the pulse of a decade, or a *look*, almost before anyone else—my *eye* was my greatest gift. I lived by my eye. And often I was criticized—ahead of my time.

And I seemed to do what I did longer than anyone. But I became involved with each new period. Long before the sixties, I'd adapted myself to the ways of youth, who were clearly taking over the culture.

So you could relate to new stars, say, Mick Jagger?

We loved each other—not carnally. But we loved what the other had. There was a fascination, a mutual one. Mick was lots of fun. He loved dressing up, and like me, he was iconoclastic in his work but somewhat formal underneath.

I've heard he's heterosexual . . .

Everyone says he's bisexual. He *wants* you to think so, yet I, who am in a position to know the truth, have never heard or seen anything which would prove it.

You took some provocative photos of the young Nureyev. It's said that older men have fallen in love with him. . . .

Or *lusted* and fell. But if you want that sort of detail, it won't be forthcoming here.

Sir, one of your own diaries—published—says that you asked Nureyev to move in with you. That you both flirted . . .

Does it? Well, then, I'm sure it does. Nobody could resist him. I was only dreaming—carried away.

Did you see him in, or as, *Valentino*, by Ken Russell?

I understand both are presented as indignantly heterosexual.

The actor and the dancer who plays him. Yeah. *Naturally* . . .

Well, I suppose one can't expect anything else.

You knew Truman Capote.

We vacationed together, often. He was a lot of fun. Sometimes.

And other times?

Too immersed in his work. To the point of ignoring other, important things. In the beginning, he was elfin and delightful. Then he became more . . . manlike. . . .

More *manlike*? You mean *manly*?

Yes. And more bulky, physically. He felt a bigger obligation to his writing, and he would forget the rest of life. He even let his toenails grow, for *months*.

Huh! In 1950 your camera captured a jumping, *young* Truman. So that wasn't the Truman Capote we know and love today?

Oh, he was just as loved then. . . .

I remember you took a photo of Pavlova's death mask. It made a personal impression, because she didn't have a typical ballerina's profile—a very hooked nose, right?

In repose . . . Well, she was beautiful when alive and dancing. But, yes, Miss Streisand could have played her—standing still. For that matter, Barbra also resembles Bernhardt, whom I'd heard she wanted to portray . . . and I did a few sketches. Just tossed them off—but there was no assignment.

I believe Glenda Jackson did that one, and it was a costly flop.

I'm not surprised.

One of my favorite of your photos was a close-up of a cat with a towel around its head. It looked so human and startled. Do you remember that one?

Perhaps Mrs. Astor's cat. Nineteen seventy or '71. I haven't done many animals.

Could you be the one Englishman who doesn't love animals? (*No response.*) Now, there's this one: a 1932 portrait of Cocteau,

with huge white hands for props. Molds? Also a column, and a bust with a mask on.

If genius is doing several things beautifully, then Cocteau was a genius. If genius is an Einsteinian specific, then Cocteau was just a very gifted artist.

The hands remind me of an outfit of David Bowie's, a few years ago, with hands—with female fingernails—at his sides. Was that a rip-off of your Cocteau photo?

Uncredited inspiration. We've all done that. Everything gets copied . . . eventually.

And **you've photographed men like Churchill and De Gaulle. Were they easier or more difficult than a Garbo or a Hepburn?**

Audrey Hepburn was a dream to work with.

Actually, I meant Katharine, but . . . well, you know what I mean.

Of course I do. *(Smiles.)* Well, politicians are *homely.* In the American and British senses of the word. They're not pretty, and they like to rule their home, their country—the world, when possible. But since they're only concerned with projecting power, not eyebrows, they are, generally, easier subjects—once they're seated before you.

Was it easy getting to such important men?

Of course! Without that kind of publicity and adulation, they're just bureaucrats. It is a notch in one's belt, to photograph a so-and-so or a thus-and-such. However, it's mutual. But they *are* boring to talk about. . . .

All right. A not-boring rumor: Did you take LSD with Mick Jagger?

I tried the drug several times, at his suggestion. And quite successfully, too. . . .

Sir Cecil! What was it like?

No, no. That would be irresponsible. I remember acutely what it was like for *me.* I couldn't describe it in general—there is no "general." And I don't want to glamourize it or make it sound safe or simple. Obviously, I stopped long ago.

In 1956 you did some memorable shots of Marilyn.

I didn't want the cleavage portraits, and I told her so. She asked her little friend Mr. Capote about me. He assented, so she came, and we posed her—with *glamour*, without that wistful little-girlishness. They're some of her best likenesses.

And in 1956 you went to work for *Harper's Bazaar*. Did you feel your artistic prime was over, or beginning . . . ?

Diana [Vreeland] assured me I had yet to blossom. I found a new setting; I had rooms in the Ambassador [Hotel] completely redone, with *dots* . . . I photographed Marilyn Monroe, Carson McCullers, whom you mentioned—she had hardly any chin, you know, like Marilyn before her operation—Hermione Gingold, and so on.

And you were still busy designing plays and . . .

And *writing* plays . . .

How many careers . . . ? You're not unlike Cocteau, whom you described as a master of several trades. . . .

But *he* wasn't very attractive. A strong face, but unusual. I don't think *my* face is unusual. Do you?

Though it became fashionable in some circles to dismiss Cecil Beaton as a dandy and an élitist, his work was long considered classic by his peers. He helped to define the periods in which he worked and lived. But when his work was honored with a massive retrospective at London's Imperial War Museum in 1974, Beaton felt morose, like "a museum relic which has outlived its energy." The year before, his beloved sister Baba died, leaving Cecil emotionally drained. And in 1974, he suffered the severe stroke which initially left his right side paralyzed and which made conversation and sustained activity difficult.

The social whirl was over after the stroke, even after Beaton had recovered most of his abilities. He confined himself to Wiltshire, receiving guests, dwelling upon and in his "nest" and gardens, reading and accepting challenging assignments. But retirement eventually beckoned, and in 1977 he put up his entire photographic output for auction at Sotheby's. This included over 150,000 photographs, 250,000 negatives, countless color transparencies, and a score of lovingly detailed scrapbooks.

He outlasted nearly all his friends, and lived to stage a minor comeback in 1979 with a thirty-page spread in the French *Vogue*. It was even said that his old ambition and wanderlust had revived. But fate intervened, and Sir Cecil survived only until January 18, 1980, four days after celebrating his seventy-sixth birthday.

Was your favorite decade the 1930s?

How did you guess?

It seems the most glamourous one.

It was the most glamourous. And dangerous . . . Who knew?

The war began a year after your prank at *Vogue*. Did that alter your perspective . . . ?

Of course. I was sorry for what I had done.

It *is* amazing, how many incredible people were alive and thriving in the early and mid-thirties. . . .

A galaxy, my dear boy, a galaxy.

What kind of man did you find attractive?

In my work, either a beautiful man with masculine qualities, or a stylish, somewhat eccentric man with a distinguished face. *Thin* men—up to a point. But if you're asking what sort of male I choose to befriend, he must merely be good-hearted.

Will you ever reveal the loves of your life?

Love doesn't translate into copies. What is important is that it be revealed from one . . . to . . . another.

Your mother's death must have affected you very deeply.

Absolutely. My greatest, most sincere fan—and my advisor—was gone.

What in particular do you remember about your mother? Or about Reggie?

My mother followed the royals religiously. But when I photographed them, she wouldn't pry—that is, inquire. She felt they were subjects—well, not *subjects*—about whom one shouldn't ask details. That was the prevalent attitude. . . . I remember that Reggie's hands were less hairy than mine were. It's funny, what one remembers.

Did you have a conventional older brother/younger brother relationship?

(Smiles shyly.) No . . . In his sexual way, he seemed older.

Did he at all resent you as the star of the family?

Don't younger brothers always resent their elders? Perhaps . . . he was envious. I like to think he was admiring. I really wanted, secretly, to please him.

Moving way ahead, as a sort of elder gay statesman, did you ever want to be part of the gay rights movement in any way?

For the most part, I admire it. But it seems largely to be an American phenomenon, tailored to young Americans' particular needs.

What are your reservations about the movement?

The loss of individuality. Understand, I offer no solutions. It *is* likely that equality can only be achieved through impersonating society's rulers. But it will be a great loss if one type of [gay] man is intolerant of another, and if conformist action, conformist good looks, ruin creativity and genuine differences and . . . individual ways of living and working.

Is there also no place for the elderly in the movement?

There appears not to be . . . unless one becomes a guru like Mr. Isherwood.

But you're much less, as they say, in the closet, than in past years.

Oh, yes. Why on earth not? By now, what does it matter?

Did it matter when most of your friends were alive?

Yes and no, depending . . . I think mostly it's to do with work.

When you're younger, you don't want to close off doors to your future development.

As a working man. . . ?

Yes. And . . . if you feel that being more honest *still* won't change people and their attitudes, then . . . why bother? I never sought to change the world, dear. I just wanted to be *part* of it, and to record it.

Through your unique eye.

Yes. Yes, through my interpretation. So I have left my own mark, without having had to *tell* people and create an uproar.

But nowadays . . .

Yes, nowadays it's healthier, in that sole regard. Attitudes *can* be changed, because there are enough dissidents from the majority's opinion.

***Sole* regard?**

Well, what *else* has improved? The world at large isn't a happier, or a kinder, place. . . .

Does the technology ever . . . scare you?

It scares us all, in terms of destruction. That's natural. But the astounding thing is how things repeat themselves; people and nations and groups of people don't seem to learn, or want to learn, from their mistakes or cruelties.

War . . .

War . . . *and* less generalized violence and repression. Poverty, of course . . .

Your photos of London during World War II certainly evoked the tragedy on all levels, from the wreckage around St. Paul's to the faces of hospitalized children.

Those photographs have not only stood the test of time, they've been particularly admired.

Do you think you were ever taken less seriously because you specialized in the beautiful people, before they were called the Beautiful People?

I don't know what you mean.

Well, as you said, Sir, your wartime photos are much admired. But you were known for fashion and film stars, for *beauty.* **The opposite, almost, of an Arbus.**

I don't know whether to thank you or get my cane. . . .

Well, George Cukor has been known as a "women's director," and he didn't do Westerns or gangster movies. And though his work is great—undeniably—he's not as highly esteemed as directors whose focus wasn't on women or . . . beauty.

The difference is also in his sexual bent. Most of the other directors—for example, Ford or Huston—are, for want of a better word, "normal."

So therefore, did you find that as an esthete and a homosexual, your work was undervalued by experts?

Somebody once said that criticism is the tax one pays for being renowned. I've caused several major stirs in my time. I don't think because I have photographed or designed things pleasing to the eye, that I have been . . . made a pariah.

I'm glad to hear it. You've taken unforgettable shots around the world. Morocco—a street filtered with dark and light, in very geometric shapes. The Ajanta caves in India.

That was a highlight of my travels. Unbelievable. India is crammed full of marvels. Almost a thousand years of fine painting in those caves. And the Jain temple in Calcutta—an Indian form of Gothic: exotic, yet starkly spiritual. I took a portrait of myself, inside the temple, amid the inlaid arabesques.

If you could have lived in another country, which would it be?

Japan. I've always been fascinated by Japan. But I'd only want to live there if I were Japanese. Otherwise, there's no hope.

What's a favorite beauty spot you've been to?

(Long pause.) Blue Harbour in Jamaica. Noel's place. It was beautiful, and there are special memories there. I took photographs of all of us—myself, Noel, his houseguests . . . one of them was Ian Fleming, the James Bond author.

Do you read books like that?

No.

You have a partiality for hats, Sir . . .

And, alas, a propensity for baldness. Earlier, when you mentioned Fred Astaire's hairline, I felt in mortal danger. . . .

(Both laugh.) How do you choose the setting in which to shoot your subjects?

I don't *shoot*, I *photograph*. Well, I've always thought it a pity that memorable personalities should be invited into a studio at all. It takes them out of their natural surroundings, which shape them, and which they have shaped. But as for devising backgrounds in the studio, I was always blessed with imagination. I suppose that's why I couldn't be merely a photographer, and I also *designed*.

You photographed Tallulah in 1929, at home—your home— holding a kind of crystal ball, with a background that looks like cellophane.

Wrong on two counts, but I won't go into that here. The ball reflected my mother's living room. I liked that. . . .

Most of your life, you've lived with your mother.

Yes, and quite happily, thank you.

And your first studio was your—your parents' home.

Correct . . . No wonder poor Reggie was always outside! He had to take the brotherly competition outside the home.

Was there ever anyone you didn't photograph that you wanted to?

Hardly. Oh: George Bernard Shaw. It's a long story, born of the man's ego. If an ego isn't practical, it's not worth a *thing*.

One of your most stunning star portraits was of Anna May Wong. To me, it's much more memorable than a Crawford or a Weissmuller.

I *did* photograph Miss Wong in front of cellophane, with a mountainous bouquet of gypsophila, which I don't suppose you've heard of. It *was* a highly glamourous and, mmm, exotic portrait. . . . Now that you remind me, T. S. Eliot never got in front of my camera. Claimed he wouldn't know *what* to wear, what kind of a collar to choose!

Why do you think T. S. Eliot was anti-Semitic, as he was known to be?

Dear boy, why ask *me* that? Why did Cole Porter detest colored people?

In those days, most whites looked down on blacks.

Precisely. Things are more liberal now, with all groups. Artists have never been immune from prejudice.

That's almost surprising to me. Out of curiosity, what did you think of James Dean?

Attractive . . . overrated. Outrageously overrated. But that seems to be a kind of recompense for dying young. Imagine if he were alive today. Or if Marilyn Monroe had lived out her life. Or, for that matter, Jesus Christ . . .

Something to think about . . . What makes you laugh?

I beg your pardon? . . . I suppose poking fun at the Mrs. Rittenhouses—what an extraordinary question!—watching them fall on their pompous bums. What makes *you* laugh?

I never know, until I'm laughing. You designed the musical *Coco*, starring Katharine Hepburn. And you attended the opening with Lee Radziwill; do you think gay men, and gay actors, will ever stop showing up at public do's with women on their arms?

Why should they?

Why should they live a lie? And in so doing, give the impression that nobody famous is gay?

I leave radical change to your generation, dear boy.

What about straight women who *use* gay men, even when they—the women—are anti-gay?

Do you mean Lee . . . ?

She's *said* she has no use for "fags," to coin a phrase.

But you see, we use each *other*.

But *she's* not pretending to be what she isn't.

Oh, it doesn't matter. Please . . . Besides, she's a friend of the very uncloseted Truman. . . .

Capote acts the way he *is*, but acting that way isn't necessarily progressive; certainly not representative.

He represents no one but himself, nor do I.

Okay, we'll move on. What, for fun, is Truman Capote's best quality, in your opinion?

I doubt if he has one left . . . Ah! I was always struck by his relationship with his friend, Jack Dunphy.

A lifemate, about whom one hears far less than Truman's society friends. What were the gay de Meyers like?

Well, it was an arranged marriage. The king had a hand in Olga's early life, always behind the scenes. De Meyer was made a baron by the Duke of Hesse, so that the de Meyers could sit in the royal box during the king's coronation. In the twenties, he and Steichen were extremely successful photographers; de Meyer was a *fashion* photographer, and he worked for *Vogue*.

Were they drug addicts?

The de Meyers partook *socially*, but I don't think they were addicts, which is a very nasty word. . . .

What's that famous story about the guests and the cocaine?

The baroness was cremated, and after her death the baron received some guests—a princess and her friend. They were cocaine devotees, and when Gayne [the baron] was out of the room, they began searching for cocaine. They found a container full of white dust, and inhaled. They were Olga's ashes.

Good grief! What a way to go. . . . Your other friend, Cathleen Nesbitt, was actually engaged to Rupert Brooke?

The war prevented them from marrying. . . . He was quite beautiful. Up at Cambridge, Maynard Keynes and Lytton Strachey used to fight over him. [Rupert Brooke died of blood poisoning in 1915 while serving in the Royal Navy en route to the Dardanelles.]

Brooke was bi, or gay?

Either or both, I don't know. But he died in his prime.

So did Mishima, the Japanese writer, who ended his own life in a most gory style. Don't you think premature death confers eternal beauty? That is, to the image?

Yes, but what good is it if one can't enjoy it?

That's true. . . . Is it true that you were responsible for much of the casting of *Gigi*?

Yes. Minnelli trusted me. His ego was very practical. He had no need to prove himself overlord, and he knew that I'd had experience with plays by Oscar Wilde—he was aiming for that kind of thing. Very pleasant to work with, he was, and the result brought countless Academy Awards—it set a record, in fact.

Someone in the crew of *On a Clear Day* told me that you even designed the *banquet* in that film?

(*Laughs.*) I do it all, don't I? In point of fact, Vincente Minnelli and I both designed the menu, with, let's see, lobsters, capons, suckling pig . . . it was a true feast.

But Judy Garland died during the making of that film. . . .

Yes, and right here in England. Minnelli was not visibly upset, but I understand he lent his daughter Liza considerable emotional support.

Were you a Garland fan?

I don't know that I was ever a *fan*—of anyone. But I thought Miss Garland very talented.

Outside of your family, whose deaths have affected you deeply?

Quite a number . . . Oh, of course . . . a few years ago, I was terribly upset to learn that James Pope-Hennessy had been beaten up and then stabbed. During the last world war, I did a book titled

History under Fire, for which he did the text. He was a good man. And a victim of *this* day and age.

Not the first gay man to die from a violent attack. . . .

Well, let's not pursue that.

Of course. What movies, if any, have impressed you?

Other than those I designed, quite a number, but only temporarily. After all, motion pictures are just shadows. I remember, a few decades ago, being very impressed by Peter Finch, by his performance as Oscar Wilde [in *The Trials of Oscar Wilde*]. I happened to mention this to Augustus John, who was asking me about the theatre, and that led to some fascinating reminiscences of John's on Oscar. He had known him, he claimed, very well. But not *that* well. . . .

I see. And what was John's judgment of the man?

Oh, he liked him. But not his . . . *"crowd."* I knew what he meant—without having to ask. . . .

Any new insights into Wilde's character?

He told me something *I* hadn't known: that a friend was ready with a boat, for Oscar to escape England and go free. But he declined; it was a friend Oscar couldn't contemplate being alone on a boat with!

Why are the famous so often self-destructive?

I've no idea. But that's not crucial, because they *live* awfully well. I attended one of Barbara Hutton's festivities, in Tangiers; don't tell *me* hers was a life of suffering.

So you did make it into countless beautiful rooms. . . .

Yes. When I worked at *Vanity Fair,* someone accused me of preferring beautiful surroundings. Of *course.*

And how did it all start—the photography, that is?

I liked attractive things, novel things. I collected photographs and postcards, even as a child. It all seemed so modern, and early in my career I was condemned for my modernistic style, where later, I was sometimes accused of nostalgia!

You taught yourself how to be a photographer?

I *was* a photographer. By twelve, I was using a wine cooler for a tripod. The bathroom became a darkroom, only inconveniencing my parents for a few years, because at twenty, my photographs were published in *Vogue*.

That's amazing. Sir Cecil, how do you want to be remembered?

I want my *work* to be remembered.

Rainer Werner Fassbinder

1945-1982

MY experience with Fassbinder was not a pleasant one. It was sad, alarming, and more than a little irritating. It was also an interview I hadn't sought, and it wouldn't have come about but for my friend Enrico Zanghi. As it turned out, I was lucky to spend time with Rainer Werner Fassbinder, though he remains almost as much of an enigma to me as when I chanced to meet him.

In early January 1982, I was staying at the Hotel Amsterdam near Place de Clichy in Paris. I'd made the trip from London mostly to visit Enrico, who'd moved there from Italy. Though we kept in touch by phone before and after that, this was the last time I saw my friend and colleague, who died of AIDS in 1984. I also went to see for myself the much-remarked Beaubourg cultural center, which had supplanted the legendary Les Halles. The edifice failed either to dazzle, delight, or distress me, leaving me—perhaps uniquely—indifferent. Enrico noted the snack bar's Moroccan workers, of both genders. Attractive, I agreed, and they spoke good French, but it took three of them to sell me an overpriced, fizzy "lemonade."

Paris has never been one of my favorite cities. Its sky is oppressively gray even in April or September. Its cold is more piercing than London's, and its people and prices are intolerable. Unlike in the rest of France (excepting "independent" Monaco). My second night, I was casting about for something to do. The cinemas were overpriced and held nothing of interest, running the gamut from Eastwood to Belmondo. I finally got through to a tourist bureau attendant, on the phone. She icily informed me that no, the fountains and floodlights at the Eiffel Tower's Place du Trocadéro would not be on tonight. *"Mais pourquoi?"*

"Monsieur, we cannot waste the energy *every* night!" I was too appalled to ask which nights they did waste.

Enrico rang up and invited me to a party at a German friend's home. "There's a guest of honor," he mentioned temptingly. "Someone world-famous." He meant, of course, Europe-famous. When we reached the place, it was so dark I had to search for a luminary; nobody was congregating around a star-turn. There was a cool blonde on a sofa, an almost-dead-ringer for Brigitte Bardot. Her sister Mijanou? *Non.* Or rather, *nein*—most of the guests were German; yet when asked what I wished to imbibe, I said Löwenbräu, for kicks, and drew blank stares. In one dim corner stood a fortyish man who looked like the stereotype of an orchestra conductor. I later learned he was a salesman for Siemens. And the blonde was in public relations with Gaumont.

But in another corner, huddled on the floor with two thinner men—well, everyone else in the room was thinner—sat a bloated man of indeterminate age with disheveled hair and extremely active fingers which were passing joints or aiding their owner with lines of coke. *"That* is Rainer Werner Fassbinder," said Enrico.

"Do you know him?"

"Not personally. I was on the set of one of his movies once. But everyone knows *of* him."

I immediately recognized Fassbinder's name(s), from *The New York Times* and certain film magazines. But I'd never seen one of his movies—and didn't, until the posthumously released *Querelle.* A *cause célèbre* in Europe, *Querelle* didn't fare so well in the States. As *The Advocate* put it, "It opened and closed quicker than a gay bar in Jerry Falwell's neighborhood."

I stared. I'd had no idea such a prolific—and therefore energetic—director would be so heavy (by contrast, Hitchcock's pace was leisurely). His bleary eye caught mine, but I wasn't sure if the distracted smile was aimed at me. I mused that most fat people tend to look alike. The distorting excess flesh gives their facial features a "jolly" commonality that to me seems sinisterly anti-individual. But as Fassbinder himself often said, he didn't look (like the stereotypical) German. That night, dressed mostly in black—including leather—and sporting a greasy, unkempt mustache, he looked more like Fu Manchu's fat brother than Germany's cinematic wunderkind.

"Do you want to interview him?" asked Enrico, who believed that no opportunity should be missed, as any encounter could sharpen one's journalistic skills and round one out as a human being.

"Rico, I'm on vacation, and I assume he is, too."

"He's only here for a day or two. About financing, I think." Enrico introduced us. Rainer murmured something in German. Enrico later declared, "Rainer hates the press."

"Well, then."

"But only if they *dress* like the press or don't speak any German. He'd speak to *you*—he's willing to speak to *me*, but you know how busy I am tomorrow."

So as not to waste his time or mine, I racked my brain: Who might publish an interview with Fassbinder back home? Most gay publications weren't interested in *foreign* gay celebrities; two had recently declined a revealing interview with a semi-closeted Swiss-Austrian-German Oscar-winner. (It later was syndicated overseas, and ran in a Japanese movie mag.) Fassbinder's open homosexuality was sure to put off most straight-edited magazines and papers, and I had no inclination to do a précis on his myriad movies with the bizarre titles.

I thanked Enrico for the offer, but bowed out. He reminded me that I always enjoyed meeting and talking with famous or intriguing people. I looked at this one and wondered. Certainly, Rainer was in no shape for a sustained chat tonight. "Tomorrow?" asked Rico. He pointed out that I'd long since seen the sights, and wasn't likely to put myself in for abuse at the hands of local department store sales clerks. "Okay," I said, "if he's really interested and doesn't mind that I haven't seen any of his films."

Enrico, whose German was better than mine, spent several minutes alone with Fassbinder, who now and then looked up from the floor to smile or grin at me. When they rose and came toward me, I suddenly wondered if the man spoke some French or English. Italian, even. Otherwise, all in German, it would be too painstaking: a dictionary in search of two talkers. "*Wie geht's?*" Rainer threw his bear arms around me, then steadied himself. "You want to interview me tomorrow at your hotel, the Amsterdam?"

"I'm sure it would be interesting."

"I *like* Holland," he said to himself. "Maybe a good omen." I didn't comment that the hotel was apparently run by a Tunisian. We met the next morning at eleven. When I asked if Rainer had eaten breakfast, he smiled mysteriously. Somehow, I thought of Dracula. . . . "How long are you here?" I made small talk and prepared my tape recorder. "Tonight only." He cleared his throat. "You leave tomorrow for Munich?" I asked. He pointed to the recorder accusingly, and said something in German, too fast for my comprehension. He got up, removed his sunglasses, and stared at me—like a child trying to decipher an adult. Finally, in English, "Your friend did not say you would use *that*." He pointed again.

Arrogance or eccentricity? Mae West, a legend in her own mind and lifetime, routinely eschewed to be taped during an interview; she reasoned that the tapes could be sold for profit. I left the recorder turned off. Much later in the day, I saw that Fassbinder's reason was paranoia.

Do the critics in Germany and elsewhere bother you?

If they bother anyone, it is the exhibitors and money men, because a misleading or negative review or attack may persuade some people not to go to the cinema and pay money to see a film I have done. I think the good critics eventually grow up and make films themselves, as Truffaut did. In America this does not often happen. I don't know why.

Do you know the classic definition of a critic? It is worth restating here: A critic is like a eunuch; he can watch and criticize, but he does not have the equipment to *do*. I do not hate critics, I am just too busy for them.

Does your prolific output make some of your colleagues envious?

I don't think a filmmaker has the time or aptitude to envy or be jealous. It is difficult to make a film, from the point of view of a producer or director, from the beginning to the end, when it is pulled from the cinemas after a short run. . . .We look at each other's work if we have time or inclination.

I think those who are envious are the critics—the more films I make, the more they have to review, and I think some of them do not like going to the movies; it might remind some of what they do not do themselves.

Which of your many films is your favorite?

All of them.

Is it fun for you to act? Or is it fulfilling . . . ?

I know what I want to express, and some projects are more personal, so I feel *I* can do it best. I may have the right look, but *more* important, the inside is right: I know the feelings.

It's been said that you're alienated from society. Are you?

Everybody is, to some extent. Even the leaders, the Establishment—they do not fit in perfectly or comfortably, so they try to remold society in their image. I am an outsider, they say, but for many reasons. To the Europeans, I am German, so outside their mainstream of what they see as morally and historically correct. To the heteros, I am an outsider. To the Americans, a European is an outsider. To the beautiful people, I am an outsider. I am not an outsider to me.

Do your films all have a gay point of view?

Not all have a gay subject, but they all have the point of view of one gay man.

Have you always been openly homosexual?

At the start, even. *(Smiles.)* But in my country, it is not so taboo. Homosexuality is not taboo in Germany, because it is seen inside the spectrum of sexuality. Bisexuality is not a new idea, not unaccepted. But the idea of politicized homosexuals is new, everywhere. In America, you have the other position: they sometimes tolerate homosexuals, if they are straight-looking, pro-Establishment—but they never tolerate the homosexuality.

It is harder to get a German man or woman to admit to or identify as homosexual, but the sexual acts, they are not so terrible, in the bourgeois German mind.

So you think Germany is an easier place to grow up gay than the U.S.A.?

I cannot tell you that, but I imagine that it is. What is harder is to be very individualistic in Germany. Do you know, among film-makers, they still deny, through ignoring it, the Holocaust? Only recently has anyone begun to explore in film the stories of any German Jews during the war. And it is the Jews who are making the push. The average German prefers not to remember.

Do you remember?

Always. When I go outside of Germany, I am reminded how such an outstanding nation could, so recently, have been taken in by such a small movement, by such small men.

Do you see a Nazi resurgence?

There are fringe groups. Affluence has brought more leisure time, more individuality, so I do not think the same conditions are here, as they were in the 1920s and 1930s. But even in Germany, there is increasing recession. I think the right-wing extremists are more of a threat this time in America and Britain.

You've criticized film festivals—or I've read that you have—yet you turn up at film festivals around the world. Do you feel they're decadent, or what?

The world is decadent. Certainly today; maybe it always was. The festivals are mostly for commercial purposes, but they pretend to appreciate high-minded political themes and intergalactic entertainments with a message. I enjoy the circus atmosphere, when I feel like a little vacation from work.

Does your relentless schedule of filmmaking ever tire you?

No, because each one is new, fresh, an exploration for me and the others. And I do for television also, and sometimes for German audiences only. Sometimes I aim to tell something to several countries. No, it is not boring or tiring, if I get to sleep.

What about financial pressures?

I do not have them. I give them to someone else. My pressures are the filmmaker's.

What about drugs? I've heard that the German drug scene—among moviemakers, anyway—corresponds to Hollywood's.

Yes, but drugs are everywhere. They are the modern relief, and some are ancient, too. Everyone does some drugs—what you call the recreational drugs. In our work, where the pursuit is creative and one tries to express what one is feeling inside, drugs are another kind of escape.

You don't believe they improve your work, do you?

No . . . I don't think they improve anything, in the long run. But they give a feeling . . . If you've tried this drug or that drug, perhaps you know this or that feeling.

Do you do hard drugs?

One reason I don't do interviews much is because I hate the paparazzi. They want the most unflattering angles, and they want to bring down those with more visibility. Don't you find journalism anonymous? I also find Americans want to know everything in my private life, about the drugs and sex.

Referring to your question about anonymity, most jobs are anonymous, on a national or international level. I don't think any journalist or writer—excepting maybe a novelist—ever chose the profession to become rich or famous.

But these journalists all want to know about the sex and drugs of the famous people.

I don't think they all do. And I think you know, because it's been mentioned by me and Mr. Zanghi, that this session may not yield a published interview.

I know that.

Well, since you did mention sex, what is your sex life like? Are you kinky, for instance?

You think now that all German gays live like in the film *Taxi zum Klo*?

No, not necessarily. That's one man's experience. But Frank Ripploh did, like you, star himself in a gay-themed picture.

His film. It was hedonistic, it did not say much about gays. It said a lot about *him*.

It's been very successful, for an independent, in America.

. . .

What does your sex life say about you, Rainer?

That I am . . . horny.

Very kinky?

I don't like to be tortured. I can do that to myself.

Are drugs sometimes a substitute for sex?

. . .

Moving right along here, do you think that gay moviemakers are better moviemakers?

Not . . . better . . . more aware. More perceptive of relationships and class systems and power in relationships on every level.

The only other internationally known German filmmaker today is Werner Herzog, who happens to be straight. Is he a good film-maker?

He *must* be—he will not have it otherwise. He is consumed by each film, but each film takes him more time, and he makes himself suffer through work. If work made me suffer, I would not do so much of it.

Are you and Herzog friends or rivals?

We are Germans.

That's it? . . . Your films have been called cynical, from the very beginning. Some titles: from *Why Does Herr R. Run Amok?* through *Beware the Holy Whore* to *Lili Marleen* and beyond . . .

How many of these, of all my films, have you seen?

Didn't Enrico tell you?

He said two or three only.

Unfortunately.

Good. Then you come to the . . . talk or the interview without a desire to interpret me through the films, or the films through me. My work is not cynical, it is realistic. Pessimistic. Life is pessimistic in the end, because we die, and it is pessimistic in between, because of corruption in our daily lives. The Hollywood-style critics who like your happy endings would think I am cynical, but in Europe, in Germany, few mention this.

You don't ever enjoy happy endings?

They're not endings. They're points in between. Everyone has . . . *some* happiness.

Why do you feel life is so corrupt?

Because everyone is selfish. I am not a saint. I am more devil than saint, if you deal in those old terms. But even those who do good will do it so it is seen, so they get appreciation for their efforts. I do not say people are evil, but today, the violence is not only psychological, as it always was, but also physical, and every part of society—everywhere—reflects this. It is still the fact that you win by playing by the rules, and the pure person doesn't have much of a chance.

Is this why your films have so many prostitutes in them?

The Marriage of Maria Braun scandalized some people because of what she had to do for success. How naive! Is Germany any different? Some in Germany believe that because of our defeat in the war we are redeemed, and that old cruelties cannot happen again, that now we are rich and happy, and we have America to protect us, so when something goes wrong, it is America's fault, not ours. Maria Braun knew that success comes faster to the one who prostitutes herself or himself.

Have you prostituted yourself in your work?

Everyone has. But some films are more commercial, and I know it. I knew *Maria* and *Lili Marleen* would be far more popular everywhere than *Fox* or *In a Year of 13 Moons*.

Doesn't that stand to reason? The first two had attractive female leads—both starred Hanna Schygulla, I believe—and the latter featured gays and, in *Moon*'s case, a transsexual.

But you wouldn't expect me to only make films with gay themes because I am gay?

That's not what I said. But a gay film usually—until now, at least—had little chance of big success at the box office.

Hollywood is making several films with gay themes. [*Making Love, Personal Best, Victor/Victoria.*]

Do you think that's a step in the right direction, or can a Hollywood picture never avoid clichés and condescension?

I have no idea. How will they portray the characters and the relationships? Will they be in the gay world, or part of the whole world, with heterosexuals and every kind of individual? The financial success will determine if it is a fad, but I think Europe is better at relational films.

Tell me something about the films you've acted in. What roles have you played?

I was Fox in *Fox and His Friends* [originally titled *Fist-Right of Freedom*]. Fox—you know the English fox races? The ones where a fox is pursued by aristocrats and royalty? I was a victim like that. A middle-class homosexual, pursued by the rich, cheated, abused, then thrown away. I played the character because it was about the typical homosexual relationship with heterosexual society. *They* control the money, the system, the power. It was a role any homosexual could play, at least the ones I know. I don't know many Hollywood-style homosexuals.

What do you mean by "Hollywood-style homosexuals"?

They act like they're not homosexuals, and they don't want to be associated with that. So they become the oppressor, outside of a bedroom.

Would you have cast a heterosexual actor as Fox?

Not unless the gay actors all moved away and I was unable to act.

What about your part in *Katzelmacher*?

I have been told by foreigners that I look foreign, not German. They picture us all as blonds, but America, for instance, is a more Nazi-looking country than Germany, if you deal in stereotypes, as Hollywood does, and you all grew up on Hollywood. The reason you didn't see more of my films—was it because they were not available, or you preferred other films or . . . why?

Foreign-language movies are usually only shown in larger cit-

ies, and I live in a small town. So I have to go and find the Fassbinder movie, usually in a smaller "art house," and most foreign-language movies only show for a week, or a few days.

I wanted to know . . . I understand it is easier to see my work in New York or Los Angeles, and most have never played in America at all.

Nope—just New York or L.A. . . . *(No reaction.)* Well, you've done a lot of movies and TV miniseries?

And also television films. It doesn't matter. Only the length differs.

Once again, what did you play in *Katzelmacher?*

I played a Greek. You know about our *Gästarbeitern* [immigrant workers]? Then you must have read of the discrimination they encounter throughout the richer countries where they work. In Germany they are isolated and misunderstood. Germany has always been xenophobic and ignorant of foreigners, more than our neighbors.

In *Katzelmacher*, the immigrant was thought to possess legendary sexual prowess, so the most envious, the unemployed, the unprogressive young Germans lynch him. Like your blacks, except that the Greek has a job, and the punks don't.

Have *you* ever been unemployed?

When I don't work, I am unemployed. Only recently has this become a problem in Germany—without work, a German male feels he is nothing.

Do they really resent sexual prowess in others?

Surveys say Germans are not remarkable in sex, only in work and organization. The young hedonists resent this.

And why a Greek? Why not, say, a Spaniard or Sicilian?

Coincidence. A good coincidence, because the Greek symbolizes ancient sex as well, and homosexuality—uninhibited sexuality and wonderful bodies.

Do you like your own looks and body?

I have to . . . Do you mean sexually? I am not handsome. I

indulge in everything . . . But the superficial power of a filmmaker is an aphrodisiac to many handsome but powerless males.

Do you feel you get asked about your sex life more often than a straight director would be?

From what I read, perhaps. They don't ask the others, not even the French.

Some of your movie titles are very unusual: *Mother Kusters Goes to Heaven, The Bitter Tears of Petra von Kant, Satan's Brew* **and** *Chinese Roulette.* **Did you choose these?**

I choose or help to choose the German titles, and now have input in the foreign translations, but some things are colloquial or cannot be translated word-for-word. Sometimes the result is silly or misleading. The *film* is important, not the title, please.

Of course. Like Ingmar Bergman, you . . .

I am not Ingmar Bergman, so I am not Ingmar Bergman.

What I was going to say is, you tend to use certain performers over and over. Hanna Schygulla is the best known to us, but also Volker Spengler, who played the male and female roles of the transsexual in *In a Year of 13 Moons.* **You obviously prefer working with familiar people. Has this always been so?**

Not always. But West German cinema is relatively small, and the good actors are few. Until around fifteen years ago, their experience mostly came from playing Nazis or Nordics in non-German films. I find Volker or Hanna are very good, very versatile, and we understand each other.

Some actors do not like to work with a homosexual director; do you know of homosexual actors who do not like to work with a heterosexual director? It is the corruption directed at those who threaten weaker souls. Others feel they must be stars, and I do not practice the star system, or treat this or that one like a wunderkind at thirty-five. Beautiful faces do not impress me. Good actors do. We become friends, they are right for a role, they grow from film to film.

Will you ever work with Hollywood stars or American actors?

Stars no, actors yes. I think there is a world to explore within

Germany, within our culture of today. We are not a small nation, and as American filmmakers explore the American experience, I explore German experiences.

I suppose this is a question not asked of heterosexual directors, but you and your mother [Lilo Pempeit] work together. Do you get along well?

Since we work, we get along. Work is the pacifier. But our relationship is not typical—of anyone. We are friends, but we give each other tremendous freedom. She is not Rainer's mother. She is herself.

Are charges, or accusations, of nepotism ever a problem?

No!

Do you make love stories?

In films . . . My work is what I love, but the subjects are today, they are German, continental. Not love stories with pretty music. When I make films about hope, it is love stories I am making. Because I do not make pretty, long-to-make films, it does not mean I am not romantic. I try for romance, but usually in today's world, one fails here.

I still put romance into films when I can, but the realities of materialism, corruption, and injustice interfere. I try to reflect how I see things, not create a fantasy world. The fantasy world is for writers and others. For politicians, too.

You've done one English-language film, *Despair*, with Dirk Bogarde, by Tom Stoppard, based on Nabokov. Yet despite these brilliant names, it was not very successful, commercially, at any rate. Why do you think?

I thought it was very good. I am pleased.

Do you read reviews or avoid them?

If they are available, if I can read them, I read them. Unless I am angry. But when a non-English-speaking European does a film in English, the British yawn and the American critics say he or she only thinks in their native language and should stick to it. I heard many reviews from the New Yorkers were pessimistic.

You said pessimism is realism.

That is not clever, because I said that part in English. . . .

Would you work in English again?

Not for the sake of it.

Who are your favorite English-speaking actors?

Charlie Chaplin? What do *you* think? I don't know. It depends what they are acting in.

I understand you also work with the same crew most of the time.

Great artists, good friends.

At a guess, how many of your associates on both sides of the camera are gay?

Some are neither heterosexual nor homosexual, and some do not identify with the gay liberation movement. If you mean who have I slept with . . .

Would you act in somebody else's gay-themed movie?

I don't think so.

Do you think your movies would be richer or deeper if you spent more time making them?

They have the depth and meaning that they have. Some people take time to make shallow films. I don't measure mine, but I know I am quicker than the others. This is the kind of work for our times—who knows how much time we have? Life is precarious. Films have to reflect the changing and fast pace of our lives. Except for the special-effects spectacles, today's films should not cost millions upon millions and take months to shoot.

The details are more real if they are not planned a year in advance. Life isn't planned that way—no matter what you plan, it usually works out another way. Time is the least thing I have to worry about, especially from those who cannot help but take more time.

You've made so many films in so few years, would you consider remaking any of them, now or in the future?

I will want to, I think, to see how time has changed conditions.

If there is another war involving Germany, to remake *The Marriage of Maria Braun* would be interesting. And if the gay rights movement succeeds in more ways than legislating new official attitudes, *Fox* will be on my list.

Your films reportedly don't feature many lesbians, at least not in depth.

Because I am not lesbian, and as you probably know, many lesbians resent a homosexual man making a film whose story is centered on the lesbian lifestyle or on one or more lesbians. Also, these films would not be very successful, and now and then I aim for larger audiences. The world of film is still with a male point of view, even in most films made by women directors.

But you do have more females, period, in your movies than most directors do.

I know women as friends, and sometimes as lovers. So I know they are not just girlfriends for the backgrounds. They have lives, too, so . . . *(Shrugs.)*

Do you generally dislike interviews because you're afraid of revealing yourself?

I think I am fairly interesting. The films I make are more interesting. . . . *(Suddenly rises.)*

During our ninety-or-so minute session, which abruptly ended with a nature-call, Fassbinder rarely removed his sunglasses. He also had a horn-rimmed pair of regular glasses, which I gathered were for reading. The man was far more intelligent than I'd have guessed from the night before, but his good English shouldn't have surprised me. His mother, by all accounts a remarkable woman, was the official German translator for Tennessee Williams and Truman Capote. Yet later I learned that Rainer often refused to speak English in front of his German cohorts, particularly on movie sets.

But though his responses—mostly in English—were fairly rapid, I had plenty of time for note-taking, thanks to the frequent pauses. At Rainer's request, I had my Sony radio on. It sat next to him on a table. He'd switched from the classical to a rock station, turning the volume up until I declared that I couldn't get down everything he was saying. Soft-spoken but seemingly unemotional, Rainer wore heavy motorcycle boots and smiled only once. Whether or not it was deliberate, he gave a robotic impression, framed by the tall, geometric window and further diluted by gray light. I'm reminded of the print ad—I forget what for—in which the man sits in front of a TV or stereo wearing sunglasses and no expression, his hair and neck scarf blowing in the wind. . . .

After emerging from the john, Rainer sat down again, but waved aside any more "interview-type" questions. As though it were important, he smiled and confessed that he'd woken up at 9:30. . . . Didn't I have any soft drinks on hand? I didn't. If he was hungry, I didn't want to keep him from lunch, but I wasn't sure if we were done. The director—who never addressed me directly or told me what I should call him—merely yawned a few times. He looked lethargically around the room, not even noticing the magazines on the small table. Courtesy of Enrico, the magazines' illustrated articles had given me a crash course on Fassbinder's colorful career.

"I'd better leave you to lunch," he suddenly said, referring to the American lunch hour. Almost as quickly as he'd burst in, Rainer rushed out and down the stairs. I turned the radio off. That afternoon, I called Enrico. "I can't say it wasn't interesting. Thanks again, Rico."

"Did he tell you a lot?"

"We didn't cover every movie—who could?—but he's had a remarkable career. A very unusual man."

"What about personal stuff?"

"Well, he's very open about being gay, but I didn't get the feeling he wanted to share his private life."

"It's not over, is it?"

"As far as I know. He left several hours ago."

"He called me."

"He called you? Are you interviewing him, too?"

"He wanted to know if you wanted to join him and his friends for dinner tonight. I won't be able."

"Why didn't he call me, to ask?"

"He's just . . . idiosyncratic."

"Tell me about it. . . . Anyway, I don't know what I'll be doing, since I'm leaving for London tomorrow after I see you."

"Anyhow, I gave Rainer your phone number, but he might stop by—you never know. If you want to stop by, there's a French

booklet I found for you on Rainer, about his background and relationships. Why don't you stop by?"

"I will."

At about six, Fassbinder called. His voice was a bit slurred.
"What are you having for dinner?" he asked.

"What, or where?"

"Can we go to dinner at eight? Can I come there and then we'll
go out?"

"Just you? What about your friends?"

"Sometimes I prefer to be alone. . . . Yes or no?"

"Yes. Come, and be my guest for dinner. What kind of food do
you like?"

"Anything. See you at eight o'clock."

He came at twelve minutes past ten, without apology or expla-
nation. We walked a few blocks to a Vietnamese restaurant where
I finally had to make up our minds about the menu. At first, Rainer
behaved normally, and he even put away his glasses. But as dinner
wore on, he began to tilt forward, then he'd jerk back and sit very
straight. He picked at his food but ordered one Coke after another.
The waitress looked at us long and oddly, which was nothing new
in un-gay Paree.

Rainer was still answering questions clearly, though less rapidly.
But his pauses were frequently, disconcertingly punctuated by the
precarious leans forward. At one point, I had to snatch his glass
up from the table; I didn't mind the exorbitant drinks tab—not
much—but I wasn't about to get embroiled in a broken dinnerware
fracas in a nonfriendly Franco-Vietnamese *boîte*.

What kind of thing makes you laugh, Rainer?

What? . . . I'm not laughing.

But when you do, what makes you laugh?

How would I know? There's not much to laugh at. I don't laugh
at bad jokes.

Do you have a good sense of humor?

I think so.

Some people say the Germans don't have the best sense of humor. . . .

Who says that?

Well, non-Germans, I admit.

. . .

You know, Rainer, I interviewed Luchino Visconti, years ago. And it's said he was an outstanding cameraman—I mean, he knew so much about the camera, and so do you. . . .

The camera is the most important way to make a movie, and I was making them when I was very, very young. *(Shakes head.)* I know everything about making a movie.

Do you have any opinion of Visconti's work?

I liked *Death in Venice.*

What about *The Damned*, which was set in 1930s Germany?

Very, very good. *(Sits up.)* No, it was very outstanding, and the characters were very unusual. I liked the colors—the orange and blood red.

And remember the green light that bathed the faces of the more reptilian characters?

The mother? The one who was raped by her son . . .

It wasn't a rape, though; she never protested. Do you know Helmut Berger?

(Smiles.)

Do you know Maximilian Schell, who's such a fine actor *and* director?

He's very, very intelligent.

I heard that *The Sound of Music* wasn't successful in Germany or Austria. . . . Why, do you think?

American musicals . . . *(Shrugs.)*

Did the Nazi subplot turn German-speaking audiences off?

I think so. That was long ago. Germans like James Bond. . . .

Do you smoke cigarettes a lot?

What?

I gather it must be a lot, because your fingers . . . excuse me, but—they're nicotined.

I smoke too much. Right now, I'm trying to cut down.

Any particular reason?

If someone around me doesn't smoke, it makes me feel a little ashamed.

Are you susceptible to, or influenced by, those around you?

Everyone is.

What do you think of contractual marriage, Rainer?

(*Shrugs.*) Marriage is marriage, with or without a contract.

You've been married . . .

Once, to a woman.

What about your long relationships with men?

. . . Paparazzi . . .

Well, may I ask why you married a woman?

What is your expression? *It seemed like the right thing to do at the time.*

Were you pressured into it?

Who isn't?

Are you still friends with her?

I married an actress. So we worked together, and . . . that helped.

Do gay actors or directors in Germany have to marry females for their images, nowadays?

I don't think so. I think the worst image is when you keep getting married, like a hobby.

Do you have any hobbies?

Work. When I'm not working, I'm with friends. . . . I like music—but loud, not from a little Sony transistor. *(Laughs.)*

Would you describe yourself as a workaholic?

Am I an addict? *(Smiles.)* I've been working less, lately.

But work is the basis of your life, isn't it?

As long as I keep working, there'll be fewer regrets.

Do you have any regrets in your life?

What would be the use?

I've read that you like fancy cars.

You have an American expression: *conspicuous consumption* . . .

What kind of food do you like?

This is very good. What's it called?

I'd have to look at the menu. Usually, what do you eat?

I don't eat so much; you think I do, because I'm fat, but I don't.

Are you dieting?

Yes.

I read that you admire American directors like Hitchcock and Douglas Sirk.

Yes. Very, very good storytellers.

Did you like *Psycho*?

Entertaining . . . but it's a right-wing movie.

How do you figure that?

The woman is punished for taking money from the upper class, and the man who is too close to his mother becomes crazy. You don't think Hitchcock was conservative?

I've heard he was anti-gay and somewhat asexual, from people

who knew him. But I suspect most straight directors are anti-gay and/or conservative.

I say it because Americans often don't know about their own directors. Tell me, is Hitch still considered English in America?

I think British-American. He's considered Hollywood, through and through. That's an interesting question; you mean that the immigrant is never allowed to forget his roots, don't you?

In most countries, including ours.

Do someone's politics influence your opinion of their work?

No, unless they're extremist-reactionary. And you?

Good work is good work—look at Vanessa Redgrave. Her P.L.O. thing is deplorable—you know, de-P-L-O-rable? (*No reaction.*) **But, anyway, she's a fine actor. . . . You know, I didn't know a thing about Douglas Sirk until I interviewed Rock Hudson.**

Is Rock Hudson nice?

Nice **is such a meaningless word. But I like him—he's very easygoing and appealing. Do** *you* **like his work, or whatever?**

He's been in some good movies. Gay, no?

Oh, yes. I was in Hong Kong last year. Went to a tailor shop, and there was a picture of Rock Hudson being fitted for a suit. I asked the Chinese tailor about it, and he said, I quote, "Rock Hudson likes *boys.*" **He meant males, of course. In fact, Rock doesn't have one age category, as so many straight or gay males do.**

I'd like to work with him.

Why don't you ask him? He hasn't done a movie in a while.

Do you think he would play a gay character, *ein Warmbruder*?

I'm pretty sure he wouldn't. Which of Sirk's movies do you particularly like?

Most of them.

And what other Hitchcock films?

Almost all of them.

Could you give an example, Rainer?

. . . I enjoyed *The Birds.*

All that pecking and . . . pawing poor Tippi Hedren. What do you think of Sam Peckinpah, or do you know of him (a director with a fetish for violence)?

I don't always like to see things like that.

You mean Peckinpah does too much of it in his films?

Ja.

Why do you think that the world's only pre-sixties gay movement flourished in Germany, before the Nazis?

German people are always liberated about sex.

Then why did they let the Nazis try to wipe out homosexuality?

They let them do everything. But, one thing in defense, they didn't always know everything they were doing and planning.

The irony is that even if Hitler had killed every homosexual male and female—utterly impossible—from five to ten percent of all new births would eventually yield homosexual people.

. . . Ignorance . . .

Are you known to be anti-Nazi in Germany, or is that completely normal, so you don't have any problem from the, uh, fringe groups?

I have trouble . . . not just politics—the politics is in my movies. Class struggle is seen as only left-wing, and also, since I'm gay, the right-wingers and the Nazis hate me. They make death threats, sometimes.

That's amazing.

It is true. Sometimes I need a bodyguard, and at my house, new installments, for protection.

Is this only recently?

I become more famous, so more threats.

Do you find that as you—or anyone—go from independent,

low-budget director to a top director with big budgets and international success, your admirers turn to enemies?

The bigger, the worse for the . . . celebrity.

In other words, they build you up, then they want to tear you down?

Pünktlich! Precisely!

Do you ever fear for your life?

No.

But then, you also got a lot of gay protest when you produced the movie *Tenderness of the Wolves,* about a vampirelike gay man who was a child-molester and murderer—a virtual Sweeney Todd. He even used their flesh as meat, didn't he?

He sold it, for that.

Well, that kind of movie's guaranteed to stir up homophobia. . . .

But it's true.

The difference between that and a true story about a similar *heterosexual* is that a movie about the straight man wouldn't provoke heterophobia—there's no such thing as heterophobia. Is it therefore responsible for anyone to make such a movie as *Tenderness of the Wolves,* particularly a *gay* man?

We cannot censor out the truth.

But choosing one subject or theme over another isn't censorship.

If we have no choice what films to make . . . *(Shrugs.)*

You have a choice, and you have a responsibility.

. . .

It's hard to imagine a Jewish filmmaker making a true film on a subject that will stir up and spread anti-Semitism. Doesn't this amount to homosexual self-hatred?

It exists. . . .

Gay self-hatred?

Yes, it exists. In many men.

Well, it's not surprising, is it? Every minority grows up with negative images put out by the majority, and every child wants to be like the rest. . . .

In Germany and all over Europe, there was much Jewish self-hatred during the war . : .

And such self-hatred is often exaggerated by a minority's enemies, offered as "proof" of the group's inferiority.

But if you don't bring this to the surface, how do you deal with it?

Well, a movie is the most public way of dealing with anything . . . Do you regret making *Tenderness of the Wolves,*—or producing it, I mean?

If I had directed it, it would have been different. But I didn't.

Do you think your movies will ever find mainstream success in America?

Has it happened with many European directors?

. . .

It doesn't matter . . . I don't want to have to change how I make something, so it can be successful far away from my own environment.

Do you basically make movies for yourself?

For me, but also so they succeed and reach people—inside the cinema, and inside *them.*

If you could have, would you have become an actor—a leading man, "Hollywood-style"?

I like being a star. *(Smiles.)* It is fun, and I like to wear clothes like a star. . . .

Stars have less to worry about, don't they?

I don't think so.

But directors have much more control—as do producers—right?

Yes. *(Smiles.)* It's good to have control.

One last Coke, and we left the multi-hyphenated restaurant. Rainer wanted to walk through Place de Clichy: "I haven't walked there alone." We didn't get there, for I steered us back. Rainer was under the influence, staggering and loping. He nearly tripped over several curbs, and his expansive gestures caught several eyes. He wanted to detour at every opportunity, and, being a large man, was difficult to steer.

I feared for his safety, what with the reckless Paris traffic, and the possibility that if he were widely recognized, a crowd might collect, and then the paparazzi . . . Within a block of my hotel, Rainer demanded, "Let's go back to Amsterdam," turning it into a sing-song chorus. The Tunisian was away from the desk, and thank God for elevators. Rainer asked for the radio to be turned on—loud—and repeatedly asked if I had any soft drinks. For the next hour or so, we made small talk, I asked and rechecked some questions, and I showed Fassbinder the magazines and booklet. These he flipped through, pausing briefly to look at some of the pictures.

Every fifteen minutes or so, he went into the bathroom and stayed several minutes. I went in once, and discovered little papers on the floor and white dust on my wooden comb. When I noted that he looked rather sweaty, Rainer muttered that he might use the room's portable-shower cubicle. I said go ahead, and he seemed tempted. Then he patted his significant stomach, winked, and decided not to.

At one point, Rainer broke the silence—I was jotting—and mentioned the subject of suicide. He asked if I'd known anyone who had committed suicide, but before I could answer, he offered, "A stupid way to say it—like to *commit murder*." We sat in silence, with the radio blaring. I waited for him to expand on his comment. Then:

So you don't think suicide is murder?

No . . . No, it isn't, because if you murder someone, you do it against his will. The victim has no choice.

But obviously one doesn't commit suicide completely against one's own will. . . .

Sometimes it's the only solution.

For who?

For somebody who is in torture. Not how long you live is important—are *you* happy?

Happy *enough*. No one's happy all the time, maybe even most of the time.

What if one is only happy doing one thing?

You mean like working?

Or anything.

Some of the people close to you have taken their own lives. Does the pain of that ever go away?

. . . *(Shakes head.)* No.

What's *your* personal feeling about suicide?

For *me*?!

Would *you* ever do it?

(Angrily.) I'm too busy.

Then who has time to talk about it? Did I read right: Did you write *plays*?

Yes. *Katzelmacher* the movie was based on my play, the first one I did.

What do you think of your fellow playwright Tennessee Williams?

He is a very great man.

What do you think of his work, of specific plays?

His work is still very good. It's more innovation now.

What do you think of his problems with drugs?

(Shrugs.) Everyone has them.

Not everyone. Don't you think people who are around a lot of drugs, people who partake, sometimes think they're average— that is, that the whole world's on a drug trip?

Everyone's on a drug trip.

Not *every*one . . . But let's quit this topic before I sound like a prude and you sound like an apologist.

A what?

Never mind. Now, you often cast favorites of yours, like Günther Kaufmann, who appeared in *Querelle*. Does this cause resentment among the rest of your cast and crew?

Why should it?

Well, why shouldn't it? In Hollywood, a producer *might* be able to get away with casting a girlfriend, or boyfriend or relative, in a tiny part. But casting a favorite in a *major* part?

No actor has ever let me down.

That speaks well for your relationships with actors, Rainer.

(Smiles.)

But, for instance, you cast Hedi ben Salim in the *lead* role of one of your films . . .

Fear Eats the Soul.

And he wasn't an actor, to begin with.

Anyone can learn to act.

And talent can be expanded upon. But you can't put talent where it doesn't exist.

It was a good film; you should see it. *Then* you would see . . .

Most of your close friends, including Armin Meier, have been cast in your films.

Let's not talk about that anymore.

Okay. Do you agree with Hitchcock, who said that actors are cattle?

He shouldn't have said that.

Do you mean he shouldn't have said that, or he shouldn't have *said* that?

Both. *(Smiles.)*

Friends are probably easier to direct than actors with actors' egos, right?

Let's not even talk about actors . . . I'm *ein* actor, too, and . . . but everyone wants to meet me just because I make movies, and so *many* movies.

Can you usually tell when people like you for yourself?

Who says they like me?

Well, you seem like a likable man.

You don't know me. How can you say that?

Your answers are pretty candid.

. . . I think this is a better conversation than an interview, but I'm bored.

Rainer began to yawn so much that I opened the window a bit to let in some fresh air. He said what he required was "something to drink," and he was going out to get some. To make sure it wasn't liquor, I suggested I go with him. But he wanted to go alone, and left. Slamming the door behind him, he announced loudly, "I'll be back in a few minutes."

After half an hour, I figured he'd gotten home. I didn't have his number to call and check, and it was too late to bother Enrico, whom I'd call first thing in the morning. But ten minutes after that, Rainer was pounding on my door. I momentarily debated whether to let him in—I could pretend I was out. But his voice was very low, and I felt sorry for him.

"What happened, Rainer? Where did you go?"

He plunked himself down on the second twin bed and groggily allowed that he'd gone for a slice of pizza. And he'd had a couple of soft drinks, and brought one back with him. "I didn't think *you* wanted any," he said churlishly. I informed him that I was going to bed now, as I had an early flight the next day (actually at three

P.M.). Rainer just grinned, then got up to turn on the radio, loud. I got right up and lowered the volume, reminding him sharply about the hour and the other guests, and reiterating that I had to get some sleep.

Like a pouting child, he slumped into the chair and feigned attention to the radio. He avoided my eyes. My irritation subsided, and I gently recommended that he take a cold shower in the cubicle. I thought that might soothe him, make him sleepy, or both. He reluctantly complied and began to strip. I kicked off my loafers and got under the covers in my clothes, turning my back to him. I heard the repeated rustle of fabric and the soft whoosh of leather, but no water running.

Turning over and sitting up, I confronted a pitiful, heart-rending sight: Rainer was quietly thrashing about and silently weeping. His socks and briefs were on, but his enormous bare belly loomed behind a barrier of clutched garments. Catching my eye, he averted his gaze and began to slowly bang his head on the wall of the portable shower. Fortunately, he soon stopped.

I got up, walked over to him, and put my arm across his fleshy back. In a split second, the vulnerability had turned to paranoid rage. "How *dare* you try to force yourself upon me! How dare you, how dare you!" He aimed to slap me, but I shifted, and he grazed the side of my head. "Get out!" I shouted. He stared at me blankly. *"Raus—raus von hier!"* I ordered. He smiled menacingly, then rushed me, stopping in mid-lunge. Hastily, sloppily putting on his clothes, he began to curse me loudly. Mostly in German—words I hadn't learned in class and wouldn't find in a dictionary. He sputtered that I was a miserable host, a lousy interviewer, and a pushy human being with lecherous intentions.

The fire in his eyes was frightening. I didn't ask him again to leave. I half-expected the Tunisian or his night porter to come knocking on my door. No such luck. The radio was turned louder, and a fully dressed Fassbinder lay down, shaking, on the other bed. Literally within seconds, he was asleep, snoring mightily. I waited a minute or two, then crept to the radio to lower it. He roused himself and barked, "Leave it!"

"The other *guests!*" I hissed.

But he was asleep almost before I finished. Lying on his back, motorcycle boots sticking out toward the window, he snored louder than I'd thought anybody could . . . Some twenty long, seething minutes later, I walked slowly and quietly to the radio and lowered the volume. He didn't wake. Back on the bed, my shoes on, I pondered what to do, once I gave up on the night porter. I could call Rico and thus wake Fassbinder and sound like a fool, or try leaving the room. But naturally, the ancient door made a groaning sound every time it was opened or closed. I could say *I* was thirsty and going for a refreshment.

Yet I hated to leave a complete stranger alone in my room, with a valuable gift I'd planned to give Rico the following day. And if I did leave the room, where would I go? I'd be welcome at Rico's, but again, pride . . . I could call him and have him phone Fassbinder's friends and have them retrieve their pet. But what if the suspicious Tunisian or the night porter—an unknown quantity—decided to take steps? Because of his Name, I couldn't risk Fassbinder's reputation at the hands of irate hoteliers and possibly the gendarmes.

In the end, I spent almost six miserable, seething hours of near-sleeplessness, sitting guard over and against my guest. Once, he got up to pee, and angrily demanded why I wasn't asleep at that hour. I refused to utter a word; he formed a hammy fist and raised it threateningly. I stared defiantly, and he cursed in German, then went to the john. When he came out—without flushing—he again scolded me most Teutonically for attempting to lay hands on him and take advantage of his "everlasting stardom."

Of course, he turned the radio up again, and several minutes later I snuck up and turned it down. We did our radio routine several times during the first few hours. But four hours into the marathon, I turned it off for good. By that hour, I imagined that even in Paris a new ruckus would fetch a porter, *some*body. I never found out . . . I must have slept more than I thought, but I was awake every half-hour on the clock.

At six A.M. on the dot, I gathered my seething anger and bounded crisply up from bed. Poking Fassbinder twice on the left shoulder, I barked, "It's time to get up! I'm sorry, but I'm leaving for the airport. Get up, please!" He was groggy, and rubbed his squinting eyes. Raising himself tentatively, he looked up at me and smiled. Then he yawned noisily. I waited for him to say something, before repeating my command—maybe a little less sternly.

"I slept well." He smiled again. "How about you?"

"I survived." I half-smiled.

Rainer got up, went to the john to pee and comb his hair, and before walking out, remembered. "Send me a copy, if it's printed!"

Rainer Werner Fassbinder died at age thirty-seven on June 10, 1982, four years to the day after his lifemate Armin Meier. Born an "ideal Aryan" on one of Hitler's *Lebensborn* eugenics farms, Meier was reportedly overly dependent on Fassbinder, who he felt neglected him. During one of Rainer's trips to Paris, Meier hung himself in their Munich home. He was found by Rainer's mother.

Earlier, one of Fassbinder's lovers, Hedi ben Salim, also hung himself, after stabbing three people in Berlin. Swiss director Daniel Schmid, one of Fassbinder's first lovers, told the press, "Rainer was an unhappy man who hurled himself into his work but had a low personal opinion of himself. . . . He could not believe people could love him. All his life Rainer thought he was ugly. . . . The basis for his new friendships was always: you are a pig and I am a pig."

The future moviemaker's early life was not of a sort conducive to lasting happiness. His parents divorced, and his new stepfather couldn't stand him. Rainer chose to live with his father, a wealthy landowner and slum landlord. It was the shy, sensitive teenage Rainer who was sent to collect the excessive rents from the typically impoverished Turkish "guestworkers" in Cologne. For most of his youth, Rainer was not close to his mother, who once took a domineering seventeen-year-old for a lover; the young man tried in vain to play stepfather to young Fassbinder.

When Rainer applied to Berlin's prestigious Film Institute, he was rejected. All his life, the M.D.'s son regretted his lack of a higher education. But although his first celluloid efforts were practically one-man shows, budgeted at around $25,000, he quickly made up for lost time. Between 1969 and 1982, he directed forty-three movies, including lengthy TV miniseries. His *Lola*, a remake of *The Blue Angel*, was, at $10 million, Germany's most expensive film up until that time. And in spite of *Querelle*'s explicit homoerotic nature, it was co-financed by the Berlin Senate—after Fassbinder signed to direct.

Besides movie-directing, the man wrote thirty-seven screenplays, fifteen plays which he also directed, and numerous radio scripts; he acted on stage and on screen, and shot, edited, and produced several of his own and others' motion pictures. Fassbinder was virtually an offshoot of his own gargantuan career, which almost single-handedly restored German cinema to its pre-Nazi international eminence.

From the 1960s on, Rainer overindulged—in booze, uppers, downers, LSD, and cocaine. He often smoked four packs a day, too, yet in his final year he would fearfully tell friends that he didn't want to die. He also told people that he envied Steven Spielberg and wanted to emulate his record-breaking success. Up to the last, several projects were pending. On the final night of his life, Rainer called Daniel Schmid in Paris and told him that he'd flushed all his drugs down the toilet—all except one line of cocaine.

Fassbinder's body was found with a burnt-up cigarette between his lips and notes on his next film under his head. There was evidence of cocaine, pills, and whiskey. A movie addict to the end, he'd been watching his video machine. It was playing *20,000 Years in Sing Sing*.

George Cukor

1899–1983

HE was one of the greatest, if not *the* greatest, of Hollywood directors. When he made his last film, *Rich and Famous*, in 1981, he was reportedly the oldest-ever working director. His career spanned over half a century, and his output of fifty movies (the first three he codirected, in 1930) probably includes more classics than any other director's body of work.

George Cukor directed his good friend Katharine Hepburn in ten films, and Garbo in two—including her best, *Camille*, and her last, *Two-Faced Woman* (1941). He directed a third of *Gone With the Wind*, and led several actors and actresses to Academy Awards for their performances in his films. He also directed practically every leading lady in Hollywood; the exceptions are few and include Bette Davis and Barbra Streisand, both of whom have declared their regret at not having worked with him.

Cukor's major achievements include *Camille*, *My Fair Lady*, *Dinner at Eight*, *A Star Is Born* (the Garland version), *Born Yesterday*, *The Women*, *Adam's Rib*, *Gaslight*, *Little Women* (the Hepburn version), *Pat and Mike*, *The Philadelphia Story*, *A Double Life*, *David Copperfield*, *A Bill of Divorcement*, *Travels With My Aunt*, and *Les Girls*.

Most of his films were hits, most were well received by the critics, and most stand the test of time. Cukor was chosen by Hollywood and Moscow to direct the first Soviet-American coproduction, the mega-flop *The Blue Bird* (with a cast headed by Elizabeth Taylor, Jane Fonda, and Ava Gardner). He began shooting Marilyn Monroe's final film, *Something's Got to Give*, which was the beginning of her end; she was fired from it, and died shortly after. Cukor's two forays into telefilms were special events: Hepburn and Olivier

132

in *Love among the Ruins,* and a remake of Davis's *The Corn Is Green,* starring the great Kate.

He worked much less in later years, but until the end, Cukor had hopes of restoring his Midas touch. His last hit had been *My Fair Lady,* in 1964. And until the end, Cukor was almost criminally neglected by his peers. The reason? Homophobia, laced with sexism. Cukor was long known—to his intense irritation—as a "women's director." He wasn't part of the brotherhood of macho, boozing, womanizing directors on the order of Hawks, Huston, or Ford. He wasn't known for Westerns, adventure-brawls, or coming-of-age-as-a-young-man stories. He never did a gangster picture.

But as he liked to point out, he guided several *actors* to their Oscars, including James Stewart, Rex Harrison, and Ronald Colman. Yet the official story of his dismissal from *Gone with the Wind* was that Gable feared Cukor would favor Vivien Leigh over him. In reality, Gable insisted that "that fag" be fired, and producer David O. Selznick finally gave in. Gable, whose first two wives were much older than he—and wealthy—had reportedly been a heterosexual gigolo who wasn't above being serviced by orally-minded gay actors. One such client was leading man William Haines, a close friend of Cukor.

In the thirties, Gable's and Haines' positions reversed themselves. When Haines was arrested in a police raid on a Y (he had another man in his cot), MGM did nothing to bail him out or cover it up—he was no longer bankable. (By contrast, MGM did save the career of a bankable—now long-married—actor in the forties, when *he* was arrested in a Y raid.) The fact that Cukor knew about Gable's former relationship with Haines shamed and somehow threatened Hollywood's King.

But despite his impeccable taste and his talent for working with actresses and actors, Cukor ruled his sets, iron hand in velvet glove. He wasn't given to Premingeresque temperament nor Fordian symbolism, but he commanded his casts' and crews' respect. Even the pugilistic Hepburn softened under his direction and usually gave in after a lively argument. "I am almost always right," Cukor would say, with a twinkle in his eyes.

Cukor won but one Academy Award, and not until 1964, a glaring oversight for a man of his talent and contributions. Toward the end, there were frequent rumblings that the American Film

Institute should have presented him with its prestigious Life Achievement Award, but it failed to do so. The last year of Cukor's life, the recipient was John Huston, a man much closer to Hollywood's all-American, all-heterosexual prototype. Many felt that, in effect, Huston was receiving Cukor's award. As one AFI board director stated, "Huston directed Bogie. Cukor directed ladies."

On the surface, Cukor was not bitter. He played by Hollywood's rules; he was never a rebel. Above all, he wanted to work and to avoid controversy. Until his final years, he was very much in the closet, although his sexuality was common knowledge in the industry, and it was known that he invited high-class male hookers to his home on Cordell Drive, directly above Sunset Boulevard. For Cukor, living well was the best revenge, and his manse was reputed to be the finest home in Hollywood. (It was copied for the set of *Something's Got to Give*, and the copy-pool was the setting of Marilyn's famous nude swim.)

In 1978 I wrote Cukor and requested an interview session. I'd heard plenty about him from some of his legions of actors, and even from some of his servants. An English friend of mine knew Cukor's Scottish parlormaid and the German husband-wife team who were his cook and chauffeur. And I once met a sometime actor who claimed to have performed sexual tableaux for Cukor's delectation. Above all, I was a fan of nearly all Cukor's movies, and more than surprised that only one major book about him had been published—Gavin Lambert's *On Cukor*.

Through reading, I'd learned a lot more about lesser directors. I knew more about Henry Hathaway, for instance, though I'd only seen a handful of his pictures. But I'd seen dozens of Cukor's. Like most of the great gay directors—including the much ignored pioneer Dorothy Arzner—Cukor was respected from afar. He was put on a pedestal by his peers, rarely invited into the real world. Much was written about his movie classics, little about the man, lest the open secret reflect uncomfortably on the men who directed Hollywood. But in his last years, Cukor increasingly spoke up, even admitting his homosexuality to a leading gay publication, in a roundabout manner.

Over half a year passed after I sent the letter to Cukor. I tried again, explaining myself fully and enclosing samples of my work. I also mentioned, this time, my age: twenty-five. A few weeks later, he called, asked if I'd be in L.A. in the near future, and set a date for me to "stop by and meet." I passed the audition, and returned later that summer for the first of two sessions, spaced two-and-a-half years apart.

What was Garbo like to work with?

She was marvelous. Very intelligent—she left it up to the director, but she had a great native intelligence.

Did either of you feel *Camille* would become such a classic?

We both liked the story. It was very romantic, and the way it was done, the way she played it, very special.

How did you feel when several clips from *Camille* were included in John Huston's *Annie?*

(*Annie*) was a contemporary musical on a large scale, and they were recalling a certain period of time, and they chose a film that has held up and been heard of by many people.

Did you take it as a tribute?

I'm sure it was a tribute.

Was Robert Taylor as good-looking in person as he was as Armand?

Yes. It bothered him, to some extent. But in the picture, it worked well for the character.

Why is Armand so often played by gay actors?

Not just actors—Nureyev, opposite Margot Fonteyn . . . I don't know. Perhaps because it's so romantic a part, and the character has a sensitivity that some actors can't put across.

Did you have any idea that *Two-Faced Woman* would be Garbo's last?

Neither of us did. But I must tell you that the studio [MGM] was trying to change her image. From a goddess to the girl next-door, a contemporary girl with an accent. The picture was a big departure for Garbo, and when it came out, for one reason and another, it was loudly booed. There were censorship problems as well. . . . She took it all very seriously, very personally. I don't think she intended it to be her last picture, but she did think, I believe, that it would be her last for a while. I think she lost faith in the studio.

It's hard to believe that Garbo wasn't that popular in this country.

She was far more popular in Europe, and we made *Two-Faced Woman* during the war, when much of the European market was closed to Hollywood films, so MGM wanted to make her more popular in the home market.

What did you think of the attempted Garbo makeover?

Then . . . ? (Shrugs.) In retrospect, it was a shitty decision.

Would you have liked to work with her a third time?

Absolutely. But perhaps she simply waited too long. I can tell you I am glad she didn't make a comeback, decades later. *Years* later, allow me to say—I don't want to make her sound antique. I understand she is still very active.

Do you still see her socially?

Yes, but we sometimes lose touch. Our paths don't cross as often as they did.

And you're the man who introduced her to Mae West.

(Smiles broadly.) Yes. That meeting has been written about so many times. Often inaccurately.

That would be one of the highlights of the autobiography you've never written.

And probably never will. *(Laughs quietly.)*

Why didn't you work with West?

It was proposed, not too long before she passed away. But it never came . . . She was very strong in her notions, and a bit outdated. Most of her directors, from what I've heard, took a lot of directions from her. I wouldn't have.

Is that why you and Streisand never worked together?

No, no. I'm sure Streisand is more pliable than Miss West was, and I've heard some good things about her in that regard. But I don't want to shatter a legend. *(Laughs softly.)*

Is Katharine Hepburn pliable?

She is not, but she is smart. We work well together, and I don't have to direct her as intensively as when she was younger.

Was she a great actress from the beginning?

No. She's had to work at it. Today, she is superb.

Were you closer to her or to Spencer Tracy?

We all worked together several times. But I know Kate better, and we worked together more often.

She stays here at your home when she's in L.A., doesn't she?

Never mind about that.

What about Audrey Hepburn?

A very professional, very charming, genuine individual.

Why did you and Cecil Beaton not get along?

I never had the intention of not getting along with him—I don't believe in feuds. For some reason he was selfish . . . tried to overstep his bounds. No team spirit.

When you were directing theater in Rochester, New York, you fired Bette Davis?

Again: no team spirit. I didn't see the promise in her that manifested itself once she came to Hollywood . . . but did you want to talk more about *My Fair Lady?*

Well, when you made *MFL*, were you aware that Beaton was also gay?

. . . *(Stares coldly.)* If he was homosexual, he wouldn't have let on. It wasn't in the air to be open about such things, then, and it wasn't in *his* nature to be open about anything. There were certain people he wouldn't speak with, on the set—he probably imagined them to be my spies! *(Smiles.)*

Why do you dislike the word *gay*, as I've heard?

Because . . . several reasons. What does it mean? Does it mean a homosexual individual is frivolous, light-hearted, or has a good sense of humor?

I'll interrupt you so I don't forget to ask a question I always like to ask. I interviewed Quentin Crisp, the author of *The Naked Civil Servant*, in London this May, and forgot to ask *him*. What makes you laugh, Mr. Cukor?

Let me think. I'm not one to do a belly laugh. Things amuse me . . . What have I just been laughing at, just now? People taking themselves too seriously. Irony, sarcasm, secrets which remain secrets and thus become more important to those who don't know them than those who do. Judy Holliday—*she* made me laugh. She could look at you a certain way, and you weren't certain if she was putting you on, but you always laughed. She could will it.

I hope that will do, for your question, because if you want everything I've laughed at . . . The older one gets—my memory is still excellent, but I have to go back further; less to laugh at, you see.

I see. Getting back to the word *gay*, I didn't mean to interrupt . . .

Ah, yes. That word. Well, it belonged to another time. Even if it didn't have the homosexual connotation, it would hardly be an adjective in popular usage nowadays. It's rather quaint. Perhaps a word like "homoerotic"—but they always object to the prefix "homo," except in Homo sapiens, and if it isn't one group that's objecting, it's another. Now you have fundamentalists who say the concept of Homo sapiens is unsound . . . . *(Laughs.)*

What is your religious background or personality?

Jewish. You didn't know? I'm old-fashioned. I still think it's best kept to oneself. I think one can have a particular background and not be devout, or a practitioner, yet still have spiritual feelings.

I'm part Jewish, and I've found that sometimes older Jews prefer to keep their Jewishness very quiet; but isn't that a result of the anti-Semitism they grew up with, particularly those people who grew up in Europe or had European parents? Your origin is Hungarian, isn't it?

But I'm an *American*.

Well, you don't disapprove of younger Jews who are more vocal or open, do you?

Not at all. But it's too late to try and convert me to activism of any kind. *(Smiles warningly.)*

Would you work with a radical activist like Vanessa Redgrave? In light of her activism *and* her anti-Israel stand?

I would work with her, but I would insist she keep politics off the set at all times. I don't approve of this mixing it all up. And I've heard she cannot be dissuaded from bringing her workers' newspapers of whatever revolution she's espousing, onto the set. No time for that. *(Dismissive hand gestures.)* Unprofessional, unnecessary, and rude.

You've worked with Jane Fonda, however, twice.

Not the same kind of girl at all. Her acting comes first—as it should. I wanted to bust her silly head, the first time I worked with her [on *The Chapman Report* (1962)].

What on earth did she do?

She wanted to rely on her looks. *(Smiles.)* She came in to audition for the nymphomaniac, but I cast Claire Bloom in that—against type, don't you see. I wanted Jane for the frigid one, and that's how I cast her. She resisted, but of course, she wanted to work with me, especially as she was starting out and had done some dreadful things.

Like Hepburn, I suppose Fonda's talent had to be brought out?

Oh my, yes. *(Laughs.)* She was used to being indulged. . . . Her father, being famous . . . I made her straighten up, and when we finished, I told her that if we worked together again, and she used the same self-indulgent methods, I'd let her have it.

And you did work together again, over a decade later.

She was a fine actress by then.

Do you disapprove of her politics at all?

Don't bother asking me political questions—I shan't answer.

Okay. What does the word "gentleman" mean to you?

(Smiles.) A male. A strong man who tries . . . I'd have to think on that one. But if you want a quick answer, a gentleman is a man who tries to live according to his own code of achievements, behavior, and beauty. Nowadays, beauty is only referred to when talking of a face or body, but it used to be an outlook or a way of life.

Most of your films incorporate the point of view of beauty.

Thank you.

I once heard that William Wyler, who's Jewish, didn't like the word *Jew*. Does that make sense?

I don't know about sense, but Willie Wyler wasn't the only one. Maybe no one dislikes it now, but I've known numerous people —Americans, Europeans—who wanted to use another word.

A less harsh-sounding word, you mean?

Possibly. It is rather a harsh kind of English word, isn't it?

"Christian," with its *s* and *n*, *sounds* gentler. The *j* sound is usually harsh—like in "Jap" or "jerk."

(Laughs.) Oh, everyone used to say "Jap." I did, too.

I cringed when I heard Eleanor Roosevelt using it, in a documentary I once saw. Her, of all people!

If you're young, you have no idea how times change.

You know the word "Jewess"? That's always struck me as rather sarcastic, or condescending.

But no one uses it now, so I don't think you need concern yourself.

I wasn't saying I was concerned, just how it struck me. . . . Has your Jewish background ever been a detriment to your career?

In Hollywood? Not as long as I did my job. There was more Jewish influence in the studios then than now. But tell me something: are you an Orthodox Jew?

Oh, no. Not a fundamentalist of any kind. Did you think . . . because of my questions . . .?

No, no. You seem proud of your background. That's good, of course. But when I talk with young people, it does—it can—surprise me how vehement they are about things. *(Smiles mockingly.)*

Vehement, perhaps, about injustices.

Since you like frank questions, what are *your* spiritual beliefs? In a nutshell, hopefully.

(Both smile.) Buddhist. Hindu-Buddhist.

You mean . . . ?

Buddhism has roughly the same relationship to Hinduism that Christianity has to Judaism. Sort of an offshoot or child that outgrew the parent. That's why I can never understand why some Christians are anti-Semitic.

Nobody should understand that, son. So what do you call yourself: a Buddhist or a Hindu?

I don't call myself. Buddhism resists labels. The basic idea is that varying religions are simply different paths to the same goal.

I like that. Since you've mentioned it, I've met several people, including actors, who were Buddhists. And I've liked them. How long have *you* thought like this?

Since age eleven . . . Before we get off religion, may I ask your opinion of "born-again" Christian influence on the media—movies in particular?

There won't be any influence of that kind in the motion picture business. They can influence television, because it goes into every home, and it has nervous sponsors. But not the more upper-crust forms, like movies, like books. And this . . . this religious revival —not just the Protestants—it's nothing new. I'm older than this century, and every twenty years or so *(Makes orchestra conductor gestures.)*, there's a new movement like this.

In the 1930s, we had Billy Sunday. He said Satan was going to conquer America. Forget the Nazis—Satan was right here, always lurking. *(Smiles.)* Mae West brought the wrath of God on her—the priests, the Protestants, the ladies' clubs. Mae got censorship going. That's the 1930s. In the 1950s, Eisenhower put "one nation *under God"* into the Pledge of Allegiance. Big protest . . .

I had no idea—I thought that was always a part of the Pledge of Allegiance . . .

(Shakes head vigorously.) You see? It's *cycles.* Now the 1970s, and you hear so much about it—you turn on the television, and on and on—but most people don't go to the pictures now, like before. Most people still don't read books. *Et cetera.* I don't worry. I just keep my mouth shut, smile and go on.

You endure.

I . . . transcend. That's an Eastern phrasing for you. Oh . . . Now, talking about this: just wait here, while I go into the library. Somebody lent me this book—wait here. *(Fetches book.)*

This is by Mishima, who was Japanese, so it should interest you. It's about these people who become all religiously involved, all of a sudden. "A *'false order,'* that tendency shared by the body and the mind to instantly create their own small universe . . . They are taken control of by one particular idea. Although what happens in fact represents a kind of standstill, it is experienced as though it were a burst of centripetal activity."

I'm glad I was able to find it. Since it's not my book, I couldn't pinch the page's corner, but I couldn't find a goddamned spare bookmark, so I had to memorize the page number. I just started reading this.

What's it from?

This is a Japanese anthology—in English, of course—of Mishima's writings. Very prolific fellow. Let's see . . . that was from "Sun and Steel," which is an essay about his art and his life and how they merged.

Now how about a movie of Mishima's life and death?

(Laughs heartily.) My dear young man, I believe about three people on the North American continent would care to go see such a picture. He was homosexual, though married and a father, he was extremely right-wing, he was a fetishist, he was Japanese, he

took his own life in the most bloody way, with his lover helping him . . .

They say *that* was the real marriage. The guy chopped off Mishima's head right after Mishima disemboweled himself.

And then the other fellow disemboweled himself. Oh, it was all very bizarre . . . and a great embarrassment to the government over there. [*Mishima: A Life in Four Chapters* (1985) has not been shown in Japan.] And now, enough of religion and ritual suicides. I will tell you, I do attend funerals religiously. Mostly as a matter of respect and courtesy, but also out of fascination for the format.

Sounds rather macabre . . .

Not at all. There's *nothing* more natural than death.

What do you believe comes after? Reincarnation? Heavenly rest? Electricity unplugged?

(*Raises arms and shakes head.*) How would I know? How would anybody know?

That's true. Don't you find it's absolutely pointless to argue about religion, or God, or what comes after death?

A waste of time, and a builder of enemies. I don't even like discussing it. So ask me about *My Fair Lady* or whatever else you wish.

Cukor's home was his castle, and when I asked if he didn't owe it to his fans, and to movie historians, to write his autobiography, he rather testily offered, "I don't *owe* anything." Gesturing about him, he added, "I *earned* all of this. Hard work, and plenty of time . . . time," he smiled, "transcended." The grounds were extensive, the garden spectacular in and of itself, but ornamented with statues, fountains, and terraces. The house was a virtual gallery: paintings by Picasso, Matisse, Tchelitchew, photographs of the galaxy of stars he'd worked with and the powerful he'd met, books autographed by authors like Isherwood, Maugham, Huxley, and Mann. And outside, the summer house where Hepburn and others often stayed. Even the parlormaid's quarters, atop the garage were deluxe, their walls hung with elegant watercolors.

Cukor enjoyed playing the munificent host. It was once said by a rival director that if Cukor could have come back as a woman, he'd have chosen to be Perle Mesta or Elsa Maxwell (rather, presumably, than Dorothy Arzner). Though he shied away from being a guest at other people's parties—especially those thrown by the baby moguls and newer stars—he was a frequent party-giver. His home was also usually open to aspiring young actors, to whom he would give almost fatherly advice. The modern, technological world didn't hold much interest for Cukor, but youth did.

The man's own habits were sparing: early to bed, early to rise, modest meals, no smoking, few spirits. But he loved the movies, and saw as many new ones as he could, often inviting young and innovative directors and actors to his home. Paul Morrissey and Andy Warhol were particular favorites, and Cukor allowed that he enjoyed "certain" X-rated films. He was a man who laughed often and chuckled even more; reminiscing was enjoyable to him, although he didn't live in the past.

But the modern penchant for sexual honesty was alien to him, and this may have been a factor in his decision not to write an autobiography. He also noted, "I'm not going to bring up scandalous stories about my contemporaries—and I've heard the most amazing true stories!" After a portion of my Q/A sessions with Cukor appeared in the gay literary magazine *Christopher Street*, I received numerous requests for information about Cukor. A year later, a French publisher wrote to inquire if I were doing a Cukor biography, and in his 1984 Gay Calendar, Martin Greif suggested that I proceed with one.

Underrated by his domestic peers, Cukor was idolized by European *cinéastes*, despite his denial that he was ever an auteur. In his eighties, Cukor traveled as far afield as Venice and China to be honored and feted. In America, his name wasn't a household word; he confessed that he'd often been confused with Paramount-founder Adolph Zukor, who lived to be over 100. But because of his classic films, and perhaps because of the incomplete knowledge about him, Cukor continues to be a cult figure.

You've been described as an open yet reticent *éminence grise* of Hollywood's golden age.

(Stares, then smiles.) All I do is answer most questions put to me.

What do you think of the tell-all autobiography?

What's suitable to one image may not be suitable to another. . . . Personally, I think if the body of work can't bring you fame, a book isn't about to make up for that.

You've been mentioned in some autobiographies, but mostly in a tangential way.

Wait. . . .

You mean that the truth will out, after a subject dies?

Yes. For legal reasons, of course.

And if it's printed that you're gay, after you're gone . . . ?

I won't care—I won't be here. *(Laughs quietly.)*

What about *Mommie Dearest*?

Joan was a contradictory girl, rather neurotic. She did ill-treat her kids, but she was on the whole a good friend to those she liked, who were mostly males.

Often gay males.

(Nods.) She helped set up Billy Haines as an interior decorator. Or is that expression out of favor these days? *(Smiles challengingly.)*

"Interior decorator?"

Mmm. That and "hairdresser." Young people don't seem to like to hear them—I never hear them saying them.

I suppose that's because of the stereotypes.

Oh, stereotypes! *(Dismissive hand gesture.)* The young spend so much time worrying about *stereotypes*. *(Shakes head.)*

Hairdressers and interior decorators were stereotypes used to put down gay men.

Where there's smoke, there's fire. . . .

That's very true. I've found that where there are rumors that someone's gay or bi, there's often a reason.

Certain actors, you don't hear rumors about, then?

That's right. I don't know why I brought this up, but sometimes people only want to see stereotypes—like in the past.

A man who wasn't heterosexual couldn't let it be known, or he wouldn't work.

That's just it—unless he were a hairdresser or interior decorator. In other words, most men who behave like the stereotype may be gay, but most gay men don't behave like a stereotype and aren't hairdressers or decorators.

It reminds me of the saying that all Parisians may be French, but not all Frenchmen are Parisian.

All Frenchmen may be French, but not all "Frenchmen" are males.

(Both laugh.) You ought to be a philatelist. Or *philologist*.

Not to mention a philanderer! Well, let's see how long a great mood can last. Do you think Clark Gable disliked or distrusted you?

Not *too* long . . . *(Smiles.)* No, if he did, *I* was unaware of it. As stars went, he was powerful, but that was little better than impotence, in those days. You refer of course to *GWTW*?

Yes. Was Gable the one primarily responsible for having you fired?

I told my version of the story at the time, and *many* times subsequently. It's amazing how much interest . . . Do you know, I was once asked to write, not my autobiography, but a book about my part in *GWTW*. If I'd been a writer, and able that way, I might have considered it, to set the record straight once and for all.

You spent almost a year working on it. It was incredibly shabby of the producer to let you go, whatever the reason.

. . . *(Tilts head slightly to one side.)*

Did Gable's animosity toward Billy Haines have . . .

That's something I'm not going to answer. Don't go too far. *(Raises a warning finger.)*

Sorry. One of Vivien Leigh's last movies was *The Roman Spring of Mrs. Stone*. In retrospect, it's ironic to watch her—still so beau-

tiful and vulnerable—playing a so-called nymphomaniac, and Warren Beatty as a gigolo who can't settle down.

Vivien was *wonderful.*

In the film?

She was a wonderful person.

What do you think of the biography . . .

I know what you're going to ask. The answer is: *trash.* Vivien was a sweet, wonderful person who had problems, as we all do.

You **don't seem to have had many problems, other than** *GWTW.*

(Laughs.) Then perhaps I haven't had. But everyone should have *some* problems. *(Smiles mysteriously.)*

You directed Ingrid Bergman to her first of three Oscars, in *Gaslight.*

Yes, a marvelous person. Good actress, but Hollywood wanted her to play good-girl roles forever. She was very earthy, funny, slightly ribald, in person. *Gaslight* brought forth some of her darker aspects. You know, she did some very good work in Europe, years later, which most people still have not seen.

Your first film as full-fledged director was *Tarnished Lady,* **starring Tallulah Bankhead. Was that rather intimidating to a new director?**

No. You see, you have to understand two things. First, I had been directing, and I was a stage manager and director. For some years. I had experience and I had confidence. When I hesitated in Hollywood—to go into directing—it was because talkies were new, and I had to study the camera and learn about motion and other things. But I got a very plum assignment, relatively early on, and that was *Dinner at Eight.* Everyone remembers it today because of Jean Harlow. But if I'm not mistaken, the top-billed star was Marie Dressler, a very big star at the time, and also an Academy Award winner from early on. Luckily, the picture was successful.

The second thing I have to tell you is that Tallulah was a charming lady—and I believe I can safely use that word. She was a

Southern lady, and in the twenties she'd been the toast of the London stage, and her later reputation, in this country, wasn't yet established. A very good actress, but her vehicles were often unchallenging. *Tarnished Lady* was not a notable success. We did become friends, but not terribly close.

She was said, perhaps not yet when you knew her, to have a voracious sexual appetite, for both genders. Did you become aware of this?

Good heavens no. And remember, it was my first picture as sole director. Another thing: in those days—and for quite a long time —I wasn't as lean as I am today.

She didn't make a pass at you?

(Shakes head smilingly.)

Actresses tend more often to have affairs with leading men than with their directors, don't they?

You might be surprised. . . .

You do have a more youthful image today. Did you consciously lose the weight?

I think you ought to know that thinner people live longer.

Is your appearance very important to you?

More so than it used to be. I do like to dress well. And I'm aware that perhaps I look better in a suit. I don't dwell on it, though.

Was Jean Harlow a vampy type?

On the contrary. Extremely wholesome and friendly. The Baby, she was called, and men and women felt protective toward her.

What could you have done with Bette Davis?

A memorable picture, I hope. But often, contracts and studio commitments got in the way. She was a very interesting actress, at the outset. Almost maniacal . . . and I did *not* fire her, the way she keeps retelling it, as though no one had ever been fired in his life! *(Smiles.)* We've *never* feuded. But there simply wasn't room for her in my group, at the time—and it was so long ago, I always wondered how she remembered, or *why*. . . .

You worked more than once with Joan Crawford.

At that time—early forties—she was rather desperate about her career. She'd already been on top and fallen from grace at Warners. We did *Susan and God,* and a rather more interesting film a year later, called *A Woman's Face.* She was very eager to please and to do well. She told me often, and sincerely, how she admired some of my earlier work, particularly *Camille.* She was a great fan of Garbo's.

Her daughter said Joan had "lesbian tendencies."

It's possible. Anything is possible.

Did you get much into your performers' personal lives, or were you curious?

There were only a few personalities I was curious about, but it was none of my business. And vice versa. Occasionally, some of the women, more than the men, would take me into their confidence, though unsolicited. A director sometimes has to play the confessor role, which I never was comfortable with, to answer your question.

James Whale, the gay British director who made so many memorable thirties films, had his career cut short by living openly as a homosexual man. . . .

You couldn't be open then . . . today you can't be if you're a performer. Producers are the least vulnerable. Older directors are next. *(Smiles.)*

Didn't it anger you what happened to a man of Whale's brilliance, for no good reason, when actors like Ward Bond and John Wayne thrived by playing bullies on- and off-screen, particularly during the political witch hunts?

(Shrugs self-consciously.) I've tried to keep out of politics. I only wanted to work. Yes. Yes, it did sadden and depress me, what happened to some of my colleagues. What could one do then? Until the sixties, almost nothing changed. If you were not heterosexual, you were discreet. I'm sure the victims were aware of this rule, but possibly it was too difficult for them to follow.

Why do you think Ronald Reagan really left the movies?

(Laughs.) Isn't it obvious? Those were *B* movies. If he'd been in *Casablanca*, he wouldn't have become governor and president. The other reason—and I don't know this firsthand—was his marriage to a successful actress [Jane Wyman]. If he'd been married to his current wife [Nancy Davis, a B actress] to begin with, his ego could no doubt have handled not being a top-flight star. People like Reagan and Lucille Ball—who was *not* a success until television— lived quite well, nonetheless. But there wasn't much of a chance for a big breakthrough.

Sal Mineo told me that if you started out in supporting roles, you usually remained in them.

Yes, yes. And once in B pictures, always in B pictures.

That's right—you never worked with Lucille Ball.

I was lucky—not in regards to Miss Ball—but I only worked with the top-flight people.

Did you ever hear that John Wayne was one of the biggest financial supporters of the KKK, back in the fifties?

I did hear something about that.

Hearing that really disappointed me. But it *was* a long time ago, and I think, in a way, he's apologized for it.

Oh? *(Sits up.)*

Well, I understand you watch very little TV, but he did a series of ads, for Great Western Savings, I believe. In them, he said that he'd made some mistakes in his time, for which he was sorry.

That's very interesting.

I felt better about him then. People with that degree of fame can rarely explicitly apologize—if they're even willing. I like to think that was his blanket apology. He had a nice personality— what we saw of it.

And remember the Panama Canal.

That's right! He was for ceding it to Panama, which Reagan completely opposed.

That was during President Carter.

Yeah, and I remember, in some shopping mall, I heard a teenage girl telling her girlfriend something like, "My mom used to like John Wayne, but now she hates him, 'cause he wants to give away the Panama Canal."

(Throws up arms in semi-disgust.) You see? How fickle they are? It's a wonder anyone in this town ever opens his mouth.

Really. Mr. Cukor, why do you think there are more gay actors than actresses?

. . . I'm trying to remember: somebody once said . . . that an actress has to be more than an ordinary woman, and that an actor somehow has to be less than a man. I'm not sure how he meant it, but it contains a kernel of truth.

Have you had close friendships with gay actors?

That is a private matter. It wouldn't be embarrassing, but it still is private, whether they are living or deceased.

Who was the handsomest actor you worked with?

. . . Robert Taylor. John Barrymore was still very good-looking when I worked with him in *A Bill of Divorcement* and *Dinner at Eight*. More recently, the chaps in *Rich and Famous* . . . the one who did the strip [Matt Lattanzi, now married to Olivia Newton-John].

Was Barrymore a terror to work with?

Ask Kate Hepburn. *We* got along, but he had a habit of exposing himself to young actresses, trying to seduce them in the dressing room. Kate was quite taken aback, I can tell you! That was the start of her Hollywood career. Eventually, they became friends.

Who was another star you directed who became a good friend?

Most were colleagues, rather than personal friends. They ran with their own packs. But Judy Holliday was a friend of mine.

Is it true that her part in *Adam's Rib* was sort of a screen test for the role of Billie Dawn in *Born Yesterday*?

Yes and no. She didn't walk through the role. It was not, as it's been lightly put, an elaborate screen test. She held her own with Tracy and Hepburn. But Kate and I had wanted her all along for

Born Yesterday, and because Harry Cohn [Columbia's chief] was so adamant against using her, we were even more determined to help Judy get Billie Dawn. However, she might well have gotten it without us, and her success in whatever role she played, before or after, was entirely her own.

Why did Cohn resist Holliday for a role that now seems so patently her own?

He thought she was fat. She was overweight, for a time . . . Cohn called her a fat Jewish broad. [Her original name was Judith Tuvim.]

But like most studio heads, Cohn was himself Jewish.

That didn't matter. He was still a bigot.

Rather like many in today's Hollywood, where gays sometimes work against gay projects.

Exactly. It's called insecurity.

What made Judy so special?

Everyone's heard the story that despite her dumb-blonde image, she had a genius I.Q. I don't know if it was that, or simply her deep capacity for feeling, but she had the talent to make you laugh and to touch you, simultaneously. She was a true clown, not just a comic. And she was a marvelous actress, but it wasn't in the air for her to change over to more versatile roles before she passed away.

Did you know that she was bisexual?

I'd rather not get into that.

I mention it because her latest biographers seem willing to deal with it, and one has said she suffered greatly for it, and that it may have been part of what she drew on to give more subtle, affecting performances. . . .

I imagine that most performers use their private emotions and struggles to a greater extent than we ever realize.

Speaking of the other Judy, do you think Hollywood deliberately withheld the Oscar that so many people felt she deserved for *A Star Is Born*?

Feeling against her was high in many quarters. Part of it was jealousy.

It seems incredible that they awarded it to Grace Kelly instead.

Well, she was a very promising newcomer, and very pretty besides. That counted for a lot, more than now.

Any other major Oscar upsets you recall?

I was very disappointed when Judy Garland didn't win, for her sake. Even though the picture was butchered by the studio [the complete version was pieced back together and released shortly after Cukor's death], she still deserved it. But one of the greatest surprises in the Academy's history was in the 1950 race, when Judy Holliday won it. It wasn't surprising that she should win, but it *was* surprising when you considered that she was up against some remarkable ladies at the height of their respective careers . . . Bette Davis in *All About Eve* and Gloria Swanson in *Sunset Boulevard*.

They might have canceled each other out.

Very possibly. *(Smiles.)*

But also, Hollywood loves a newcomer—do you think it's a mania?

Consider this, if you like: a newcomer hasn't had any failures yet. . . .

Did it hurt, that you were overlooked for so long?

I'd been nominated, but never won. And it didn't mean so much to me, I didn't think, until I won it. I did enjoy receiving one.

Finally.

Yes, finally. *(Smiles wryly.)*

But then, Garbo never won one.

Exactly. *(Smiles broadly.)*

You worked with Anna Magnani, whom I especially like watching. Was she difficult?

That word . . . *(Clasps hands.)* I think most artists are difficult in one way or another. Miss Magnani was highly opinionated, but wonderful to work with. The effect often justifies what precedes it, as I might say it did with Marilyn Monroe.

By the way, you were offered *Cat on a Hot Tin Roof,* **weren't you?**

Turned it down because without the homosexuality it made no sense, and they wouldn't do it *with.*

But it was redone for television, with Robert Wagner as Brick, as Tennessee Williams wrote it.

Yes, recently. A vast improvement . . . considering.

Considering that it didn't star Elizabeth Taylor and Paul Newman?

(Smiles assent.)

You directed Marilyn in *Let's Make Love,* **and I liked her performance, but Yves Montand was his usual wooden self.**

It might have been Gregory Peck, instead, but he insisted on first billing, and so did Marilyn.

By now everyone knows that Montand had an affair with Monroe, although he was married to Simone Signoret.

He was very involved with Marilyn, and I don't know if that didn't dampen the performance he might have given.

You've said Marilyn was maddening to work with . . .

Yes, and I'm not the only one.

Tony Curtis made a disparaging remark that kissing her [in *Some Like It Hot]* **was like kissing Hitler.**

That's going too far—ungallant.

I interviewed Tony Curtis recently; he wouldn't talk about the past.

What else has he got?

A book—he wrote a Western novel.

I'm surprised. *(Smiles.)* Was he pleasant to interview?

Yes, and he used a lot of big words and wasn't bitter at all; sometimes it's best to avoid the past, don't you think?

(Laughs, then starts to get up.)

I didn't mean you! *(Both laugh.)* Anyway, that had a lousy ending, because the magazine that assigned the piece didn't think he was an interesting enough writer—after all, it's only his first book—so I wound up using part of the interview in a round-up about actors who are writing novels or autobiographies.

Did the first magazine pay you off, though?

Sure. A kill fee.

Well, that's good. Walk away with dignity, and always get remuneration.

Were you paid handsomely for what you directed of *GWTW*?

That's not a very nice question.

I'll try not to mention money again.

Too many actors are trying to do other things . . .

Including directing their own movies?

Shit, yes. And writing, for heaven's sake! . . . This round-up of yours, what did it appear in?

A magazine called *Bookviews*. I'll send you a copy.

I've seen it; I read it. Now, I suppose you want to know more about Monroe. They always do. *(Smiles.)*

You've heard of Ken Murray, the man who does the home movies of the stars? I saw a segment—years and years ago—of him hosting some movie premiere, the first one Marilyn attended. And when he got her to come up to his mike and talk to him, he wouldn't hardly give her a chance to speak! And he kept making her into a joke . . . Very embarrassing to watch.

I think I've seen that. It *was* long ago. . . . But Marilyn grew used to dealing with that—more adept. Though she never changed her approach, did she?

Do you think *Something's Got to Give* could have been a great film?

No! It could have been a fine commercial comedy [Dean Martin and Cyd Charisse were to have costarred]. What remains, on film, of Marilyn is charming. She was at her most beautiful (in a costume test). But it just wasn't meant to be.

Were you surprised when she died?

It always comes as a shock, even when sometimes you can imagine it beforehand.

The script was eventually turned into a Doris Day picture. What did you think of it?

I wouldn't like to say.

Back in 1935, you worked with W. C. Fields. All these wonderful people. What was *he* like?

A not very happy man, but a great comedian. It was *David Copperfield*, and some of the people there got a kick when Fields would badmouth the juvenile lead, Freddie Bartholomew. He called him a sissy, and worse. Behind his back; I presume Fields never told him to his face. I would hope not! He could get away with it, however. I couldn't have, if I'd wanted to.

Who was the worst actor or actress you worked with?

(Smiles.) You know, five years ago I wouldn't have answered that. I'm not sure it's fair to say . . .

The whole world isn't gonna read this.

(Winks.) One of the most unpleasant working experiences I've had was with an actress called Anouk Aimée [in *Justine*]. That picture could have been much more than it was allowed to be.

You took that one over from another director.

Yes, but I'd done that before, with far better results.

I've seen Aimée in several Italian and French movies—so chic and alluring. What was wrong with her in *Justine*?

Attitude. Intractable. Like Marilyn, but without the results. Let me tell you, that girl knew she'd probably never work in Hollywood again, or she'd never have defied me like that.

She's strictly in European movies, isn't she?

She belongs in European movies.

My Fair Lady **was so highly publicized at the time; when I was in third and fourth grade, it seemed like you only heard about two movies—***MFL* **and** *Cleopatra.*

That's true, and it's also interesting, because both actresses [Hepburn and Taylor] received a million dollars for their roles.

Were they the first to earn one-million-per?

Possibly Brando did first, in *Mutiny on the Bounty*. You could look it up. Which of the two did you prefer? *(Smiles.)*

Audrey Hepburn was my favorite actress at the time, but I loved ancient Egyptian history. . . . Both were remarkable pictures. I've heard that *Cleopatra* **was supposed to be two movies—one about her and Julius Caesar, one about her and Mark Antony.**

Mankiewicz virtually disowned the result, I believe. Elizabeth did, I know that. So now the film historians are talking of finding the missing footage and coming up with an endless epic.

Or the original two movies?

Yes. I don't know if the public will care, but it's very gratifying to a director.

Today, looking back, are you satisfied with *MFL***?**

Yes, quite. It wasn't done on location—not at all—but too many pictures done on location aren't as authentic or atmospheric as they could be. We don't necessarily need locations to create a time or place or ambience—look at our work from the 1930s and 1940s. And that was a problem with *Justine*. There was also the problem of a child-brothel, which couldn't be shown with any reality, even in 1969. Yet the studio knew it was in there, and that it would be shot. We had to use *dwarves*.

Now you see teenage actresses playing teenage prostitutes. *Justine* could be done much better today, particularly with a different cast of major performers.

One of the performers was Michael York, of *Cabaret* fame. Didn't you have some censorship. . .

Yes, yes. Too much Michael York would have shown, and so on. Fucking kibbitzers, those censors.

An endangered species, nowadays.

Not endangered enough!

Yet you've said that there was more sex within the Code than without it.

Well, the Seal—it signified approval, you see—did mean that somebody with a dirty mind had at some point gotten involved, and made people redo something the audience might not have seen as dirty . . . so that it came out dirtier, by implication.

The censorship-boomerang, eh? Would you recast any other of your films?

I've been remarkably lucky. I don't think so.

Jack Warner wanted Cary Grant for Professor Higgins!

And he could have pulled it off, but it would have been another picture. Of course, with Cary's star-pull, they could have retained Julie Andrews as leading lady, which it caused quite a furor when they didn't. But as it happened, Rex Harrison was splendid, and so was Audrey Hepburn.

Basically, all Warner wanted was a box office name, then?

To insure a hit. Record sums had been spent, even before production.

I hope you don't mind this question, but if the top-billed star had been Grant, rather than Hepburn, do you think *you'd* have been hired to direct?

I directed Cary Grant several times.

What I mean is, if the top star weren't a woman . . . since you were thought of as the prime director of actresses . . .

How tactful! *(Laughs.)* I understood your question the first time. Sometimes it's smart to play dumb.

So is it a yes or a no?

An I-don't-know.

One of your efforts which is now something of a minor cult film is *Les Girls.*

(Smiles.) Do you think it could possibly have to do with the title?

I wonder. Do you regret *The Blue Bird?*

It's like a war: you learn from it and hopefully mature, thanks to the experience. At least there weren't any casualties—human . . .

It was the second time Liz Taylor almost sank 20th Century–Fox.

But not the same circumstances as *Cleopatra.* Not at all.

And how did they figure that *The Blue Bird* was a remake of the Shirley Temple movie of the same title?

I'm supposed to be the expert? *(Smiles.)*

Jane Fonda played Night, Cicely Tyson played Cat . . . If Jane was Night, who played Day?

Well, not Miss Day. There was no Day. But there was Light; Elizabeth Taylor played Light, among other roles.

I read a few reviews . . . I understand the musical highlight was a song called "The Blue Haloo." What's a haloo?

(Sighs, mock-yawns.) It had to do with Light. Elizabeth sang that song.

Oh . . . And Ava Gardner was in it—I don't remember as what. How did she and Taylor get along?

Splendidly. They knew each other from when they were all in Puerto Vallarta, doing *The Night of the Iguana* for Huston.

Since you mention him, what do you feel when you hear—not rumor, but their own statements as proof—that a director like Huston or an actor like Harrison is homophobic? Does it have any effect on you?

(Shrugs impatiently.) I'm not going to applaud them, but . . .

that's life. Just let me add this: there are many people in this business who say they don't like homosexuals or blacks, as a whole. But they're nice to one or two of them, on an individual basis.

Well, there's still no basis for looking down on a group. I think it's indefensible. It's disappointing, is what it is, whether the bigot is a star or not.

I agree; it's disappointing. And that's the extent of it.

Yes, usually. I haven't read Graham Greene's *Travels with My Aunt*, but I saw the film. Wouldn't Katharine Hepburn have been too old for it?

(Shakes head emphatically.) She would have been closer to the right age than Maggie Smith was. Of course, due to illness, she had to back out, and *I* would have, but Kate insisted I stay with the picture.

You didn't want to work with Maggie Smith?

No, no. I admired her work in *The Prime of Miss Jean Brodie* tremendously. But I felt an obligation to Miss Hepburn.

Which actress would have done the character more justice?

I don't like such comparisons. Perhaps Kate would have been less mannered. . . . It doesn't matter now.

What do you think of TV movies?

Some are very good. More important, I think you can tackle significant topics there that you can't do in features now. . . . You can't spend those unbelievable millions of dollars on something too risky for the kids who make up most of the movie audience now.

Yet look at *On Golden Pond*, which has brought adults of all ages back into the theaters.

It's a very good sign.

Why haven't you done more television? Your few efforts there have been outstanding.

Thank you. I doubt I would have attempted them without Kate. Now this sounds snobbish, and it's not meant to be, but I am not a television type.

Could you elaborate?

The characters and sometimes the performers on television tend
to be . . . smaller. The pace is too quick, and I'm not exactly a
slowpoke . . . The network may have its own ideas, so may the
sponsors, the pressure groups. There's just a lot of bullshit—*movie*
executives are more far-removed from a picture's set. But on the
other hand, you can't really knock television—no use!—and for
the future, who knows?

**What sort of significant topics do you think you could do for
the small screen, with or without Ms. Hepburn?**

Something in the vein of *Golden Pond*, possibly. Or—*you* brought
it up—something like the newer *Cat on a Hot Tin Roof*, meaning
an adaptation of a classical work.

A classical gay work?

Well, yes.

It was often said that, starting with the 1950s, George Cukor
failed to keep up with the times. Along came Brando, discontent,
franker themes and, in the sixties, homosexuality. But Cukor's
pictures didn't reflect the changing times, beyond *The Chapman
Report*, which was inspired by the Kinsey sex surveys. After *My
Fair Lady*, he made only one more sixties film, *Justine*. In the '70s,
he did two features and two telefilms. Then 1981's *Rich and Famous*,
a more contemporary story starring Jackie Bisset and Candice
Bergen.

Why didn't he work more after *My Fair Lady*? There's never been
a satisfactory answer. A possible solution is that once the swingin'
sixties happened, the clash between Cukor's refined sensibilities
and his reticence on the one hand, and all-out-openness and risk-
taking on the other, proved stymieing. His detractors said that
Cukor too often judged his movies' success by their box office.
Indeed, popularity was one of his—and most directors'—self-confessed goals.

But the key to the director's artistic conservatism may lie with
the 1935 film *Sylvia Scarlett*, which starred Katharine Hepburn—
mostly as a boy—and Cary Grant. The picture was a big money-
loser for RKO; producer Pandro Berman informed Cukor and Hep-

burn (but not Grant) that he never wanted to see them again. The offenders offered to do another picture for RKO, *gratis. Sylvia Scarlett* had been a daring departure for its time, and for Cukor. He never again dared so boldly, and avoided gay or semi-gay themes more rigorously than most straight directors might have. Time softened his judgment of *Sylvia Scarlett*, now considered a classic, and eventually allowed him to direct a *Rich and Famous*, in which the nudity was entirely male. Alas, *Rich and Famous* was not the hoped-for hit. But Cukor was, by then, willing to talk more freely and honestly about his career, gay topics, and individuals—about which and whom he was almost never asked. He would talk, in fact, about almost anything except himself.

Would you call yourself a modest man?

How . . . ?

You don't like to talk about yourself much.

No, no. What for?

What has your relationship with the press been, over the years?

There wasn't one, for the most part. Nobody was interested in interviewing directors, and they still don't give a damn about producers, for which I can't blame them entirely. *(Smiles.)* Then came, you know, the French, and their auteur theories. Even then, I didn't have many reporters battering down my door—for better or for worse. *(Smiles.)*

When do you think we'll see a book, or anything major, written on Dorothy Arzner?

It does surprise me that nothing's been done so far. But women directors are only beginning to become . . . popular. It isn't in the air yet. Someday, I think a girl writer—one of these feminists—will try and do a book about Dorothy.

I notice you still say "girl" or "lady" for *woman.* Is that just force of habit?

I can change it, if I have to. *Woman,* instead of *girl.* But I still like *lady* best.

The male equivalent of that is *gentleman*, yet that's rarely used now, is it?

Not among anybody I know. *(Smiles.)*

Now, going back to *Sylvia Scarlett* . . .

(Mock-groans.)

It wasn't one of your numerous hits.

Indeed not! It was a low point for me and for Kate Hepburn. At one point we actually thought we might not work again—she in particular.

That was well before *Some Like It Hot*, before cross-dressing was fashionable in films. But why such vehement reactions against the film?

Audiences will accept a heterosexual male character in drag, but not a female who is convincing as a male, and Kate was very convincing as a handsome young man. She was a male for much of the picture, and a minor female character grew fond of her. Audiences were very cold to that. It was a major disaster for us.

But when you say vehement reactions, it was the studio that was that. Audiences weren't furious or indignant, really, they were just aloof to it. Didn't give a good goddamn.

Would it have worked if it had been Cary Grant in drag, instead?

No. Not then. Some years later, Cary did do that [in *I Was a Male War Bride*]. Today, it could work very well, but probably not with a female as male. It would depend on the script and, of course, on who was doing the impersonation. It helps if the performer has a particular image and then tries to reverse it.

But this new film, *Victor/Victoria*, with Julie Andrews, looks promising.

Yes, yes. That's true. And of course, Miss Streisand has been working on Singer's *Yentl*, so that'll probably make a big dent in what I've just said. *(Smiles.)*

***Sylvia Scarlett* was made after censorship and the Code came in, yet you got away with Hepburn in drag for most of the movie.**

But . . . we had to add a silly, frivolous prologue, to explain *why* this girl was dressed like a boy, and being so good at it. We weren't allowed to give the impression that she liked it, or that she'd done it before, or that it came naturally. Because the critics, who were a tad kinder than the studio executives—well, who wasn't?—kept saying how suitable the drag was to Miss Hepburn.

I'll bet she liked that.

She *did*. *(Smiles.)*

Let me get this in order: your first breakthrough as a movie director was *What Price Hollywood?*

No!! *Dinner at Eight*. I was in seventh heaven—and determined to stay there!

***What Price Hollywood?* was really *A Star Is Born*, yet it's never mentioned today. Who was in it?**

The female lead was Constance Bennett. Very charming girl. Very popular at the time. A charming woman, too. *(Smiles.)*

Yes. But everyone now thinks of the Janet Gaynor vehicle as being the first *A Star Is Born*.

And that one's very much out of the limelight, next to the Garland and Streisand pictures. *(Shrugs.)* But never mind. *What Price Hollywood?* is a good picture.

***Dinner at Eight* was a huge hit for you. Shortly followed by *Sylvia Scarlett*. A big hit, then a flop. So why was your reaction so nervous?**

(Bristles slightly.) They were just starting to say that I had the Midas touch—maybe they *shouldn't* have said it. Maybe *I* shouldn't have believed it. But *Dinner at Eight* was a major hit, well thought of, everyone loved it. Then *Sylvia Scarlett* drew such wrath from RKO . . .

But wouldn't one expect more wrath from homophobic, bottom-line-thinking studio executives than from critics or an average audience?

Yes. Yes, but the studio paid our wages, gave us our assignments, controlled our working lives.

And some of your private lives.

(Smiles ruefully, then brightly.) Private Lives . . . yes, now I see that we overreacted. But I was new to Hollywood—Kate was new—and . . . *(Shrugs.)* I've never disowned that film. Now it's a cult picture, and I can see it was very much ahead of its time—made today, with a young Kate Hepburn, it would be a hit.

But it doesn't always pay to be ahead of one's time. . . ?

(Slowly shakes head.) Not *usually*.

Out of curiosity . . . .

(Laughs.) Of which you have plenty!

You, too! *(Both laugh.)* **Out of curiosity, said the cat, what did you think of Cary Grant's suit against Chevy Chase, who referred to him as "a homo" on Tom Snyder's show?**

The "Tomorrow" show? I thought it was a tasteless, foolish thing of Mr. Chase to have said, and Mr. Grant had every right to sue. [The case never went to court.]

Irrespective of whether a performer is or isn't gay or bisexual, he or she has the right to sue, you think?

Yes, because it may or may not be true, and because the individual may not want it known, if it happens to be true, and even if it is, it's nobody else's concern. Besides which, the effect on one's reputation or even career is invariably detrimental.

As long as non-heterosexuality is made to seem a stigma, it won't change. Though it's slowly changing now. But when a public figure—and I'm speaking in general, not of anyone in particular—who is gay pretends to be straight, it *is* other people's business, because the message they're sending is that it's still not okay to be gay, to be what you are. That's an appalling message to send to young people, of whom some five or ten percent will realize their gayness anyway.

Yes, I know what you're saying. And it's true. All I know is, *I* wouldn't want to be the one to sacrifice my career to the New Honesty.

No one should have to sacrifice their career. But with so many

gay or bi stars and directors, etc., there's no reason to tolerate such mindless and unnatural conformity, and the frustration it brings.

It's easier to be honest in one's maturity.

Yes, I imagine past fifty or sixty, it isn't going to destroy one's career. Yet not one big star has publicly come out.

They tell you in interviews, don't they?

Oh, sure. But they understand that no magazine is going to run their quote—or if it does run in a gay publication, hardly anyone non-gay will ever know about it. These things don't get picked up, reprinted.

There's much more of that printed in Europe. But it doesn't get into print here much. . . . I think someday some relative—probably an ex-wife—is going to call the shot and reveal that so-and-so is really homosexual.

The only way out of the Hollywood closet is to be dragged out?

(Nods.) And with these tell-it-all biographies, I think it's only a matter of time.

Do you think a lawsuit would . . .

(Gestures no with hands.) Cary Grant sued because it was television, which everybody watches. But if, as you should know, it's something, about somebody else, in a paper or magazine, they're not going to sue. That would only magnify it.

Of course not. An editor of mine once got a complaint from the gay husband of an actress I'd interviewed. Both had hit TV series at the time. Anyhow, he was irate about a phrase his wife had used—a phrase that normally doesn't imply gayness. But she did say it, and it was on the cover of the magazine.

He didn't make legal noises, did he?

Not at all. He was just jumpy. But the editor—who told me about it after the fact—told him that they hadn't printed a fraction of what they could have printed.

(Laughs.) What does it matter, anyway? But several magazines do that; it's a love-hate relationship with the stars who sell their copies for them.

I've read about *Confidential* magazine, in the fifties, which didn't last long, because of what it reported or made up about stars' private lives.

That was almost as big a scare in this town as the Red scare. But the most angry ones were the actresses with the virginal reputations!

There was a lot of gay innuendo, too, though . . .

Oh, several names, including Rock Hudson . . . He'd gone out with starlets, then actresses and stars, but he'd resisted walking down the aisle.

I always heard it was his agent, Henry Willson, who pressured Rock into getting contractually married.

But why do you think Willson pressured him? He was getting so famous.

Much more pressure on men, wasn't there? No one ever pressured Greta Garbo, I'll bet.

Not really—not that we know of.

Ironic that Cecil Beaton came closest . . .

Did he? *(Sarcastically.)*

He's a fascinating man. Like you, he's lived in the same beautiful home for ages.

Well, he's a very social man . . .

As are you. You've probably thrown birthday parties for dozens of movie stars. I was always crazy about birthday parties—attending them, I mean.

I'll invite you to the next one I give. But it's not always actors . . . You know, movie stars aren't always the liveliest people; I think that in many cases, the camera robs them of something.

Like those natives in Africa?

Not their souls, but something in the personality. There are several movie actors who refuse to *shine* unless they're stood in front of a camera.

Home movies might be a solution.

Yes. *(Laughs.)* I gave a birthday party for Ethel Barrymore . . . in 1949. That was a lot of fun . . . Hmmm. *(Closes eyes momentarily.)*

It's astounding, you could remember one party in 1949. . . . Sometimes I have trouble remembering what I ate for lunch yesterday.

(Smiles.) Ethel Barrymore isn't a tuna-fish sandwich.

You've introduced so many stars to Hollywood, or gave them their first big break. Like Jack Lemmon—you directed his first movie, didn't you?

Yes. *(Distracted.)* It starred Judy Holliday.

You gave Shelley Winters her first real part, in *A Double Life*, with Ronald Colman.

For heaven's sake, let's not have an entire list. Yes. *(Smiles.)* I did bring a lot of young people onto the Hollywood screen. I like discovering fresh talent, and I've always liked young people. I've envied them—their looks, vitality. . . .

Well, when it comes to energy, you've been very prolific yourself.

Thank you for reminding me. But the truth is, I never felt myself to be a young person, the way most people are young. I was always old for my age.

And now you've outlasted practically everybody. Does that give a certain satisfaction, or is it just sad?

It's just the way it is. The lone oak in the forest. I don't . . . I don't take pleasure in seeing even my, shall we say, depreciators pass on. But each birthday is . . . a quiet triumph.

Someone else who had great drive and enduring artistic vision whom I got to meet was Luchino Visconti.

Ah, a very fine director.

Were you friends?

I'm *here*, and he was always working in Europe. But whenever we visited each other's turf, we would get together. Have you seen many of his pictures?

As many as I could. It's not easy . . . but maybe once some of them get on videocassette. What do you think of Visconti's work?

Very, very original and worthwhile. So many fine pictures . . .

He made certain actresses—like Claudia Cardinale—famous. But he was better known for working with particular actors repeatedly. Like Helmut Berger . . .

I saw *Conversation Piece*, their last picture together. It was very unusual . . . stunning. Did you see it? An unforgettable nude scene: Berger . . .

Frontal?

(Nods and smiles.)

What did you think when Pasolini was murdered? It was almost right after I interviewed Visconti; while I was in Italy that time, somebody had asked if I were interested in interviewing Pasolini.

Were you?

I'm sure I would have been, but I didn't know much about him. I heard about that crazy film, *Teorema*, where the handsome young stranger comes to the house, and all the family members fall in love with him—even the maid—then go crazy.

Hilarious! But you should have interviewed him.

I think it was a theoretical question, not an invitation. Someone told me he only did interviews with "politically committed" journalists.

Well, it was terrible [the murder], but he went out of his way to offend the authorities. Who knows what really happened . . . That's how it goes.

What did you think when Sal Mineo was killed? No one knew what to think, for a while.

That was tragic—very, very tragic. Ridiculous Fate . . .

Did you also know Sal?

Yes, long ago.

Oh . . . ?

Quite long ago. *(Clears throat.)*

Of course, the most grisly star-murder, I suppose, was Ramon Novarro, with those two brothers.

That made me very upset.

Kenneth Anger gave all the gory details in *Hollywood Babylon*.

Not all of them . . . But *(Shakes head.)* don't ask me. It was brutal. Bestial.

They ransacked his place and destroyed priceless objects, just to find some cash.

I don't want to go into all that, it's repulsive. But I worked with Novarro. Gave him a part in *Heller in Pink Tights*.

I remember that, with Sophia Loren as a blonde.

Yes. My only Western, as it were. Novarro was still good-looking—he was an exotically beautiful young man. In the twenties, he was almost as popular as Valentino, but he had far more class. I believe his family in Mexico were aristocrats.

How interesting. Did you know Valentino?

Do I look *that* ancient? *(Smiles.)* I knew Alla Nazimova, the stage manager of his marriages.

To lesbian women?

I believe so. One of them—Rambova—was Alla's lover. Alla had many distinguished female lovers, including our Dorothy Arzner and Oscar Wilde's niece, I forget her name . . .

Dolly, wasn't it?

Yes, yes. Dolly Wilde . . . Did you know that Alla Nazimova was Nancy Reagan's godmother?

You're kidding?! Nancy Reagan's godmother was a lesbian?

(Smiles.) I'm afraid Alla's claims to fame have diminished. . . . After her death, she was best remembered for the Garden of Allah, the hotel built, or remodeled, from her fabulous home. Now *that's* gone.

How do you feel about stars like Elton John or Joan Baez who *come out*?

They're very courageous . . . but I can't help thinking it's somewhat exhibitionistic . . . I'm from another school . . . Until the last few years, I was never asked why I didn't marry.

What was your response to that?

(Shrugs.)

Did you ever come close?

I don't know. I'm not sure I can remember that far back.

Were there one or two great romances or relationships in your life?

I don't know. It would be embarrassing to reach so far back.

Do gentlemen never tell?

Gentlemen don't. Besides, who would care? I'm an old man now.

Would you direct a gay-themed motion picture?

How do you define that?

A film in which one of the two or three major characters is homosexual, inclusive of lesbian.

Isn't it curious that female homosexuals want a separate word for themselves, but there are no separate adjectives or nouns for female and male heterosexuals? You with your interest in words, do you know why?

No. I ought to ask some gay women, or lesbians, why. . . . So would you direct a gay film?

Perhaps something in the manner of *Victor/Victoria*, but . . . I don't know. I try to direct things of interest to the public at large. With today's economics, you have to appeal to a broader group; a specialized "hit" is not a hit, and if your last picture was financially successful, it's far easier to get the next one off the ground.

Is it difficult for an older director to get backing from the baby moguls?

That's a marvelous term! Well, you know, much depends on the project—the script and the stars, and then the director. Past achievements . . . they don't count for that much, where several millions are involved.

You took over *Rich and Famous* from another, younger director.

They're all younger . . . I'm the George Burns of directing—a friend told me that one. *(Smiles.)* At any rate, Jackie Bisset was involved in the production end, and she had certain ideas, and so I came into it.

Did you like the outcome? Did its box office disappoint you?

I was pleased. What do you think? Did you like it?

I enjoyed it, and I liked the combination of Bisset and Bergen; now I'd like to see the original [*Old Acquaintance*], with Bette Davis and Miriam Hopkins.

Some reviewers called it a female buddy-film. Miss Bergen was very funny. Both ladies enjoyed the working experience, and it was something of a departure for Miss Bisset.

It was your most erotic film, with the sex-in-the-airplane-john scene, and the nudity, all of it from young men. Was all that your idea?

Not initially. But it made a point; the sex and the nudity all occur in the context of the Bisset character. She was somewhat promiscuous, where the Bergen character was more circumscribed in her sexual life and her work.

At the end, when Bisset wants to give Bergen a kiss, Bergen asks if she's queer. She seemed to repudiate that side of their relationship, and that could be interpreted as homophobic, after all they'd been through.

So many things can be interpreted on different levels, but no. I disagree. In fact, it was an acknowledgment of an undercurrent which was never openly expressed. It was bound to be in the air, after so many years and shared emotional experiences. Don't you know of same-gender heterosexual friendships in which there's a strong attraction? It doesn't have to be sexual to be romantic.

Are you a great believer in romance?

Oh, yes. But then, it was part of my background, my work, the Hollywood I worked in for so long. Now it isn't fashionable, but it may come back.

Is current gay culture the last bastion of romance in America?

I think part of it is, but there's the darker side of getting all the sex, all the kicks possible. I don't disapprove, but I think it eventually is tiresome.

Did you have many censorship problems during Hollywood's heyday? I mean, more than other directors?

No more than anyone else, and perhaps I wasn't focusing on that aspect of things . . .

Have movies influenced the sexual revolution?

I think the contrary. Eventually the pictures mirrored the changes in society. Hollywood is not very up-to-date, even now.

Paul Newman has been trying to launch a film of the gay novel
The Front Runner. **Why couldn't you do that?**

With Paul Newman, perhaps I might. They tend to want younger directors for these controversial things.

I've also heard that gay-themed films are seldom allowed to be directed by gay directors.

Entirely possible. In Hollywood, that makes sense.

That they feel a gay director wouldn't be impartial, even though heterosexual directors direct hetero-themed films, and female directors seldom get to direct anything but so-called women's pictures.

Why don't you type that up, photocopy it and send it to the studio heads? *(Smiles.)*

What's your next project, Mr. Cukor?

There are several I'm still trying to launch.

Does any of them have a gay theme, perchance?

Not as yet.

Do you have regrets about your career—either what you did or didn't do?

Very few, and very private ones.

Would you have banned the "women's director" label?

That I would have. If I could have. Even "ladies' man" sounds better.

Any regrets about your personal life?

Ah! Now that, I wouldn't say.

If you were starting out today, would your work and your life have been very different?

Without question. Absolutely. You younger people often forget how much our times mold and influence us. But I wouldn't have changed my times for any others, even if I could have.

Rock Hudson
1925–1985

R OCK Hudson was one of those
bona fide stars who was more memorable than any of his more
than sixty films. Most people would be hard-pressed to name more
than a few Hudson vehicles, the most famous being *Giant* and
Pillow Talk. His looks and productivity were his trademarks, not
the typically unchallenging roles he played. But then, as Hudson
was the first to admit, his talent was relatively limited. When star-
maker Henry Willson asked Roy Fitzgerald if he could act, the ex-
truckdriver said no. But Roy was tall, willing, and splendid-look-
ing. Willson renamed his strapping starlet after the elements: the
sturdy Rock of Gibraltar and the durable Hudson River.

Hudson debuted in *Fighter Squadron* (1948), but went nowhere
fast. Early titles included *I Was a Shoplifter*, *Peggy*, *The Fat Man*, *Here
Come the Nelsons*—which introduced Ozzie and Harriet—and *Gun
Fury*. Director Douglas Sirk saw promise in the Universal contract
player, and starred him in several fifties films, starting with *Has
Anybody Seen My Gal?* (1952). Hudson hit the big time in 1954, in
Magnificent Obsession, with Jane Wyman; they reteamed the follow-
ing year in *All That Heaven Allows*. The 1956 classic *Giant* earned
Hudson his sole Oscar nomination. His costars included Elizabeth
Taylor, James Dean, and Sal Mineo—there were rumors of affairs
with the latter two.

One of the Sirk-Hudson collaborations was *Written on the Wind*
(1957), based on the life of heiress-singer Libby Holman. In it, Rock
resists the persistent advances of sexpot Dorothy Malone. Rainer
Werner Fassbinder said of the character, "He's the most pigheaded
bastard in the world. How can he possibly not feel something of
the longing Malone has for him?"

Hudson's roles were frequently women-chasers, women-haters, or both. He represented a two-dimensional male archetype intrinsic to the 1950s, and so he worked constantly, toiling in mostly forgettable pictures. Box office prominence began with the then-racy "bedroom comedy" *Pillow Talk* (1959). It was the first of a string of comedies—three with Doris Day—pairing Hudson with a bevy of leading ladies. Through the mid-sixties, Rock Hudson was a household word, firmly entrenched in the closet, with an arranged marriage (to Willson's secretary Phyllis Gates) in his dossier. The closest he ever came to a gay role was in *A Very Special Favor* (1965), in which his character faked disinterest in "girls" so as to eventually seduce his psychiatrist, Leslie Caron.

In the mid- to late sixties came the antiheroes and the talented ethnic actors, nearly all of them shorter, more "real-looking," and more true-to-life than Hudson's screen persona. Such flops as *Darling Lili* and *Pretty Maids All in a Row* helped tumble the unfashionable star from box-office grace, and in the seventies he made the transition to television, top-lining in "McMillan and Wife" and various miniseries. The eighties brought open-heart surgery, an unsuccessful second series "The Devlin Connection," a few miniseries (he played the U.S. President in "World War III"), two feature films (the second one, *The Ambassador*, so far unreleased) and a stint in TV's "Dynasty." Ironically, his final professional appearance, on Doris Day's pet cable series, was presented by the officially homophobic Christian Broadcasting Network.

In 1975 I met Rock Hudson at his Coldwater Canyon home, through a San Francisco businessman who'd known Rock's former lover Tony. We met a few times over the next couple of years, at Rock's home and in mine, in San Mateo, several miles south of San Francisco. Rock would now and again repair to the Bay City for rest and recuperation, meeting with gay friends and visiting gay nightspots. Apart from bathhouses, Rock didn't frequent gay hangouts in his own backyard of Hollywood.

In 1977, Rock was in between movies and miniseries. To his great relief, "McMillan" was a thing of the distant past. That year, he finally agreed to let me interview him, at his home, by the pool. It was more of a conversation than an interview, and he agreed to touch upon a few gay topics, knowing that anything really revealing wouldn't find its way into print. Nonetheless, it was to be a franker interview than most of the ones he'd grudgingly granted over the years, usually to promote his films. "With all the comings-out and the unwed star mothers in the seventies," he confessed, "I can breathe a little easier. I don't have to pretend as much." The spotlight once trained on him had dimmed, and Rock was increasingly frustrated by having to live an open secret.

The interview was rejected, however. "Too risky"—not because of Hudson's reaction, since I'd given him a good idea of what I would and wouldn't include, but because of reader reaction. "We don't want to rob our readers, who are mostly housewives, of their cherished illusions." A standard interview-profile finally ran in *Movie Stars*, in two sections. "You see? America just doesn't want to know," said an understandably cynical Rock—not that my first version had been any kind of coming-out piece. Even so, the published result drove a wedge between us, through no fault of my own: *Movie Stars* cut any mention of *Avalanche*, focusing entirely on Rock and his past. But with or without publicity, Rock's new movie went into a box-office deep freeze.

We didn't meet again until 1982, although in the interim I saw him perform in the hit musical *On the 20th Century*, at San Francisco's Orpheum Theatre. I also saw him in a West End theater lobby while he was in England making his penultimate movie, *The Mirror Crack'd* (1980). It reunited him with Elizabeth Taylor and was set in the nostalgic fifties. In early 1982, Rock called me from L.A. and said he'd like to get together the next time he was in San Francisco. He apologized for the *Avalanche* misunderstanding; I noted that a friend is rarer than an interviewee. But he urged, "Go ahead. You can interview me. It might be fun. For old times' sake."

"No holds barred?" I teased, fully aware that in 1980 he'd again denied his homosexuality, to the British press.

"Boze," he laughed, "you know I'll bar any questions I don't hold with. Besides, who's gonna publish this anyway?" So he detoured to San Mateo. It was the last time I saw him.

I didn't know *Magnificent Obsession* was a remake of a 1935 picture.

Sure it was. It had Robert Taylor and Irene Dunne in it.

Robert Taylor . . . Did you know him?

I met pretty much everybody. But the guy I'd really wanted to meet when I came to Hollywood was Jon Hall. I used to love watching his pictures.

Who was Jon Hall?

He was in a lot of stuff with Maria Montez.

Oh, yeah: *Cobra Woman*. By the way, who won the Oscar the year you were nominated, for *Giant*?

Old Baldie [Yul Brynner]. *(Smiles.)* And if he hadn't won, it would've probably been Olivier.

James Dean was nominated too, right?

So that let both of us out . . .

Did you *really* want that Oscar, or is that a dumb question?

I wanted it, but Yul Brynner was in all kinds of things that year, so . . . I wanted it, because it would mean I could put *Taza, Son of Cochise* behind me forever. *(Smiles.)* That naked little man tells the whole fuckin' world you're a big success.

You're a Midwestern boy, right?

Winnetka, Illinois, is as far from Hollywood's bright lights as you can get.

A Scorpio, right?

A November man, tried and true. *(Smiles.)*

How do you feel about birthdays and aging?

I welcome birthdays. I relish them, as a matter of fact.

One of your recent birthday parties was covered by a fan magazine which said you wore a T-shirt with an unprintable slogan on it. Something sexual?

Very sexual . . . only close friends attended, but someone from the fuckin' press sneaked in. I don't think it's important, either, to quote the T-shirt.

People might not understand?

People never understand.

Would you call yourself a discreet man?

You learn to be discreet.

Getting back to growing older, do you feel different or better now than as a young man?

I'm even comfortable with my gray hair and this paunch! I don't let it go too much, though; I work the paunch off for pictures.

Even Paul Newman has a paunch.

(Laughs.) Yeah, Paul's a little paunchy, even though he doesn't eat desserts. Popcorn's his dessert—one of them. . . . But I do— I do look forward to the future. I have confidence, and I hope to see the year 2000. Though I don't know about being seventy-five . . . I have more time now to do personal things that my schedule didn't allow for, before.

Were you always confident, or were you a shy movie star?

Being a movie star does make you rather paranoid. When I was younger, if someone made a gesture toward me—even said just *hello*—I wondered what they wanted. It was easy to be paranoid, and I found it difficult to communicate with people. Often, I wouldn't say what was on my mind, or speak up when something or someone interested me.

Like what or who, for instance?

I was interested in music, books, art. But I didn't want it known because it would be considered sissy stuff. Back home or California, same thing. I had one image—and the name that promoted it— but my interests were . . . diverse.

I'd have thought someone so tall and handsome would be brimming with confidence.

It never works out that way, does it? Only stupid people are confident at an early age. Don't you think that's how it works? I was self-conscious about my height—to me, over six feet was a giraffe. I wanted to be shorter, where most of today's actors are shorter, and want to be taller. I wanted to be like everyone else.

You don't still yearn to conform, do you?

Less and less. Today, I love my height, among other things. But it takes time. There just ain't no shortcut . . .

What about the marriage, and how do you feel about contractual marriages in general?

Without going back to the ashes of my own experience . . . if someone wants to sign the contract, go ahead. But I think having kids is the only reason for marrying, nowadays.

Did you ever want to have a son? Or a daughter?

Not enough to have one. Obviously. Now I'm too old, especially to have a son. A boy needs a father, and the communication just wouldn't be there—too big a gap. I'd be too old for him to relate to; it's tough enough with a twenty-year difference. Same for adoption. I got asked about adopting, a lot. But it wouldn't be fair to the kid.

Do you get lonely or depressed?

Of course. Lonely . . . depressed—who isn't, now and then? Try picking up a newspaper; it only seems to get worse.

You're one of the few Hollywood stars who hasn't had psychiatry. Is it because you're a loner or very well put-together upstairs?

Just upstairs? *(Chuckles.)* I'm not a loner, actually . . . I think if you have a couple of good friends, then you talk to *them*, and psychiatry isn't necessary. They have a better motivation to do right by you than a stranger does, whatever his degree.

In some cases, there's also the problem of finding a non-homophobic shrink . . .

Yeah, somebody you can trust, whose own head is screwed on straight.

Do you enjoy long conversations with friends?

I don't know about that . . . thirty minutes' worth of talking, and maybe nothing gets said. I'd rather laugh with them, or toast the sunset with a cold, fresh martini.

You've been to George Cukor's house, of course. He doesn't drink much.

No, but he's a perfect host.

I think at the 1959 Academy Awards presentation, you did a duet with Mae West of "Baby, It's Cold Outside." Is it true she never, ever drinks or smokes?

Don't you believe it! She doesn't smoke. . . .

Rock, was it hard to reach fifty? And what about sixty?

Don't rush me, don't rush me! Sixty is a big one—I won't even think about that yet. But fifty was not really crucial. Forty was, and thirty-nine was, because I was approaching forty fast. But now I don't have to push; things have fallen into place, and my fifties have been the best part of my life.

How about professionally?

Now I know and accept my limitations. I guess I always did, but now . . . as I said, I don't push so much now. I have more patience, too. I can enjoy music freely, I can be philosophical—it's great.

You've turned to the stage, doing musicals—a true challenge for someone groomed as a movie idol—with Carol Burnett, then On the 20th Century . . . Your generation of Hollywood stars simply didn't appear on the stage. Why?

We were too pretty, it was felt. If there wasn't a close-up, wow, what a waste! And it's scary, appearing live. But it's worthwhile, and I've enjoyed it. It got me beyond my previous limitations.

Then you have none now?

Hold on, now. I'm not Olivier or Brando. In movies, there's so much I can do . . .

Part of the problem seems to have been that you were only cast as a leading man, and there wasn't much depth to such a character.

In many cases. But some of the comedies were enjoyable.

Did you prefer the dramas or comedies?

I've done so many dozens of pictures, I couldn't categorize like that. How do you compare *Magnificent Obsession* and *Strange Bed-fellows*?

Would you have worked with Ms. Lollobrigida a third time?

I've learned patience, but I'm not a saint.

Well, *Come September*, with you and her, was one of my favorite comedies, as a kid. Nancy Kulp—Miss Jane of "The Beverly Hillbillies"—was in that.

I hardly know Nancy, but she's pretty nice.

Everyone thinks you did umpteen pictures with Doris Day. Yet you only did three.

Yeah. Why don't you put that in the headline: He Only Did Three with Doris! Set a lot of people straight.

Some of those pictures with her had very homophobic sub-plots. . . .

Yes. *(Tenses.)*

Nick Adams, who was also gay, was the butt of anti-gay humor in *Pillow Talk*. How did you feel about that then, and today?

Then, I just did my job. Now, I don't watch it . . . I don't sit around watching what my friends call pieces of the Rock.

If you had it to do over, would you have conducted your career the same way?

How the fuck should I know?!

I didn't mean to get you angry.

I'm not angry at you, it's just a damned silly question.

Now that films are being reevaluated from a gay perspective, as in Vito Russo's book *The Celluloid Closet*, do you think—

Dammit, what's done is done. They're right, and everyone knows they're right: movies were anti-gay. Movies *are* anti-gay. And movies will *continue* to be anti-gay.

So one does nothing?

No, not at all. But what's the use of pointing out what's already finished and done? Spend the time agitating for the future, or something more constructive like that.

Well, without understanding of the past, it's hard to understand the present, or to correct the future. And homophobia is so insidious that often people—straight *or* gay—don't realize when they're watching it. Do you think people brought up in Nazi Germany always realized, *ever* realized, they were watching propaganda in the movies, on . . . Oops—I almost said television.

(Both laugh.) This program is brought to you by Nazi soap . . .

But you're *for* a positive gay image, aren't you?

Well, who isn't?

But it doesn't just happen—it has to be made to happen.

And even then it doesn't happen, for some people.

Do you feel people should be sorry for closeted movie stars?

You mean because they're stuck?

To some extent, they're stuck. . . . On the other hand, they live like kings.

Horny kings.

Yes, horny kings. They *are* better off than the gay construction workers, who don't have mansions and limos to comfort them.

Man, what on earth are you trying to say?

***You* tell me.**

I think you're trying to get me to apologize for being famous, or for being a star, or for being . . . myself.

But not for all three.

(Both smile.) I know, I know. It's a damned shame, but this is . . . the way . . . it is.

You don't think coming out of the closet is easy, or worth it?

Easy?! The more people it affects, the more difficult it is. I'm sure it's worth it to some people.

But you live pretty much the way you want to . . .

So why upset the situation?

If a star about your age, and your stature, came out, do you think he wouldn't be hired again?

I'm not sure. He could make a living on the lecture circuit—all kinds of nuts do that. But I wouldn't see him getting hired to do a miniseries.

If you were offered a non-stereotypical gay role in a classy motion picture, say directed by George Cukor or scripted by Arthur Laurents . . .

Produced by Ross Hunter . . .

Yes. Would you do it?

In a movie, huh?

In a movie.

I might. I don't make as many movies as I did. What's floating around isn't inspiring enough for me to haul my ass out of bed for two, three months.

Is that because of the youth market of today?

Or am I over the hill?

You're not, are you?

Not for television, and television's more damned conservative than it has been in years.

I can't totally agree, when you consider some of the things put on—certain telefilms, topics on sitcoms and dramas . . .

This Falwell guy's pretty popular.

But he's a small part of the picture. You have more daring material, more gay material, than ever before, too. I mean, there are so many more channels, and options.

How would I know? I just watch "The Doris Day Show" all the time! (*Laughs.*)

I liked that. You know who I really liked on it? What was his name?—Billy de Wolfe as Mr. Jarvis, the fussbudget neighbor. He was priceless.

An old queen from way, way back. Billy was great—he could break up anyone.

Never contractually married, did he?

Nope. As *The New York Times* would say, "a confirmed bachelor."

You know what Lily Tomlin calls it? "Shy." She says, "In the fifties, there were no gay people—only shy ones." With a smile —you know the sly way she smiles.

I think she's fabulous, one of our biggest talents.

Now give me an idea about this: are you politically liberal or conservative?

Have you heard, either way?

I've heard conservative—from conservative people.

Make it middle-of-the-road. You?

Yes, but depends on whose road. The middle of Hitler's road or Falwell's road is still conservative.

Are you a politics nut?

As opposed to a health nut? No. But entertainment is politics.

How long did it take you to find that out?

Vito Russo's book helped; it shows clearly how the movies we were reared on, the movies we all watch, are mostly propaganda, as much as entertainment.

Have you interviewed Doris Day?

No. How come?

Just wondering.

You like her, don't you?

Great girl.

But I've heard you don't particularly like to socialize with her.

Not that I don't like, but we don't socialize.

She retired from films in 1968—the same year *The Killing of Sister George* came out.

I heard Doris was offered the lead in that. *(Smiles.)*

As Sister George?! I couldn't see Doris as a butch stereotype. Yet I couldn't see her as Mrs. Robinson, either [Day was offered the female lead in *The Graduate*].

Doris is probably happier out of the movies. . . . Yeah, a whole lot came out in '68. *(Laughs.)*

Would you ever retire from films, say at sixty-five or at sixty?

What for? What on earth for?

Would you appear nude?

Come on—you know I did [in *Embryo*]. You mean in the future? Yes, from behind, at a good weight.

What about from in front?

(Smiles.) They'd have to charge double admission.

More talent than we suspect, eh?

More than some suspect . . . Next question, please.

Your career revived, or took a new turn, with "McMillan and Wife." How come you put the show down so often?

I'm honest. Usually. The program was terrible—probably why it was so successful. Television's a monster, it eats people and unoriginal ideas.

The money was great, I'll bet.

Television's a bottomless pit of money. But no one ever said it had good taste. When they wanted to go [with "McMillan"] to two hours, I said, "Why two hours? The thing doesn't hold up for ninety minutes!"

How about the much-discussed sequel to *Giant*?

People in Hollywood do a lot of discussing . . . mostly.

Is Liz still a good friend?

Elizabeth hates being called *Liz*. . . . We're friends.

I don't think any major star has had as many gay directors,

scriptwriters, costars, and male friends as Ms. Taylor. Why is that, Rock?

She likes men around her. Even if it's just one, and even if it's platonic. I don't think she has many girlfriends. . . . She's a romantic, and with men around, she can have the illusion that it's romantic, but without the hassles.

I see. You re-teamed in the Agatha Christie *The Mirror Crack'd*. Was that a good experience?

It was. Old times; it was even set in the 1950s. Tony Curtis and Kim Novak and Geraldine Chaplin were also in it. It was fun working in England.

Now I'll tell you something you don't know. While you were in England filming, I was in London. Wanted to see *Rose*, the hit play with Glenda Jackson. Sold out. So I waited in the queue one evening, for cancelations. And out of this big car, steps a woman, her husband—I'm assuming—and then *you*. It's crowded, but you walk into the lobby, tall, silver-haired, with your glasses on— you towered above everybody.

How did you know it was me? *(Smiles teasingly.)* Lots of people say they see people who look just like Rock Hudson.

Bullshit! *(Both laugh.)* I'd know *you* . . . And I remembered reading in *Variety* that you were in England making the picture with Liz . . . Elizabeth Taylor. I felt like going up and saying "Fancy meeting you here." But I didn't.

Did you get in?

To see *Rose*? No. But I did see her years later in another West End play—where she played Eva Braun, instead of a schoolteacher.

(Reaches to put hand on my shoulder.) You poor kid. I could probably have gotten you a pass.

Oh, don't be silly. Anyway, the next day I called British *Photoplay* to see if they were interested in an interview—*then* I'd have gotten in touch with you.

Did they want an interview?

Oh, yes. With Elizabeth Taylor.

That figures. Poor Elizabeth has nothing new to say—*hates* the press—and I have a million things I've never told the press. *(Laughs.)* I hate them, too. *(Smiles.)* Did you see anything else that night?

Yeah. *No Sex, Please, We're British.* **It was amusing, but really like an English version of** *Three's Company.* **In a situation like that, in the lobby, were you aware of how eyes gravitated toward such an imposing figure?**

That becomes part of your skin. Like having a mole on the right—or is it left?—shoulder. I don't try to attract attention, but my height alone does it, and some people say I'm good-looking, to boot. *(Smiles.)*

How was Glenda's performance that night?

Great—anything she does . . .

I think so, too. Why not do more high-quality work in Britain? You're at least as popular there as here. You could do stage, television, films, with people like Glenda or Maggie Smith.

I'd love that. But they don't think of me in that context. I'm old Hollywood, not old Art, darling. Maybe that'll change; it's one reason I let the hair go gray.

It looks terrific.

You know what they say about flattery . . .

How do you feel about your most recent films?

Expletive deleted—no comment!

You've done a lot of two types of movie: the all-male-cast kind with a military or other butch theme, and the vehicle for Rock Hudson and a major actress.

But the plot's the main thing, see. Whether it's an ensemble kind of thing . . . I did something called *Twilight of the Gods,* with Cyd Charisse. A whole bunch of us, at sea, me in charge—but we didn't *go* anywhere. Now it sails around on late-night TV . . .

You did the all-male *Ice Station Zebra,* **which was Howard Hughes's favorite film. He watched it daily, I read.**

That could drive anybody crazy, even a billionaire.

You've worked with most of the top stars. Less so, recently. Or have the personalities changed?

We still have strong male personalities, and men dominate the box office lists. I was at the top of those lists, oh, back in the late fifties, early to mid-sixties. There were female heavyweights all over the place: Elizabeth, Doris, Julie Andrews, Audrey Hepburn, Natalie Wood, on and on. Now it's just a few, and they work less often, by choice, in spite of those women's rights changes.

Types change, but Mia Farrow or Susan Saint James—they're no substitutes for Susan Hayward or Lauren Bacall.

I did a picture with Mia, *Avalanche*. But those disaster flicks aren't so hot now. Everything's going to kids in outer space, though TV now and then comes up with something surprisingly good.

What about the gay-themed TV movies like *That Certain Summer*?

I've watched them. They have a point to make, because most people don't know beans about the subject. Of course, TV's nothing but compromise, so you can't expect a real hard-hitting gay picture made for TV, or shown on TV, intact.

Would you star in one?

Not at this point. You'll notice that established names can't really be seen in those things.

Not in "those things," but in feature films—people like Olivier, Brando, Peter Finch, Mastroianni, etc., etc.

Foreigners.

What about the batch of gay-themed films, like *Making Love* —and *that's* getting plenty of publicity—that are coming up?

I'm for it. I think, from what I gather, *Making Love* will be a kind of breakthrough, even if it doesn't make a fortune. Though I hope it fuckin' well does.

Does playing straight ever bother you?

I'm always playing, hopefully, somebody other than myself, so

I'm used to it. It's a job . . . I'd like any role that would stretch me, where I was credible. But I'm not about to drag myself up in leather or in chiffon, and that's where that aspect of Hollywood stereotypes is at, at the moment.

Did you know Sal Mineo?

Yep.

And Gary Cooper, no doubt. *(Both laugh.)* **Where did you know Sal from?**

We dated a few times.

And speaking of leather and chiffon, you knew Paul Lynde fairly well, didn't you?

Mmm-hmm. What's he got to do with . . . ?

He was on Hollywood Squares, and they asked him some question like, "What's a biker's biggest concern?" and he said something like "Whether chiffon goes with leather or not." I've heard he was a lonely man?

I've heard it, too. *False.* He had a good, long-time friend.

Do you prefer long relationships?

If they're not . . . constricting.

Are you monogamous?

I can try to be . . .

What about groupies, of both genders?

I'll take on the male ones, you take on the girls.

So groupies have a chance with you?

It's happened a time or two. *(Grins.)*

Sal Mineo and I discussed how stars don't usually have affairs together.

You mean they take things into their own hands? *(Smiles.)*

But you and . . .

(Raises a warning palm.) Hold it, hold it. There's someone I'm not going to talk about, and you know who it is, without asking.

Jim Nabors.

Sal Mineo told you big names don't mix, was that it?

Yes. Do they?

Sure, sometimes . . . But, um, you want to be careful about your name, so you get your own circle of friends. . . .

Does that include hangers-on and sycophants?

It did. I don't keep anyone around me who isn't genuine—no acts here. Out *there*, okay, but none of these closeted kids who think they're *possibly* bisexual. *(Mimics a Valley boy.)*

But some people are bisexual.

Really? Name two.

Two?

See? Bisexual just means you pay for it. *(Grins.)*

You've been attracted to a woman or two, haven't you?

Or three or four. So what? Every guy's been attracted to a high school math teacher or a coach. Big deal. That's not a sexual thing—it's just a damned attraction. Most bi's are just bullshitters.

It reminds me of the story of the bat—not quite a mammal, not quite a bird, just itself, and so when war came, no one wanted the bat on their side.

Where the hell did you hear a stupid story like that, Boze? *(Laughs.)*

Pardon the expression, but fuck you! *(Both laugh.)* **I heard it from my high school math teacher—no, English teacher. Come on, there *are* bisexuals.**

Okay, okay. If you're asking am I one, I'll go that route—good public relations. If it's good enough for Gore Vidal and Elton John, it's good enough for me. I am bisexual, happy and proud. A woman in every bed . . . and a man, too. Satisfied?

Fulfilled. (Both laugh.) **I don't think we'd better continue this interview. Most of it will never get published . . .**

So long as it's in Japanese, who gives a shit?

Or in *The Advocate*?

(Smile fades slightly.) I'd give a shit about that. . . .

But seriously, folks . . . You know, Rock, you smile much more in person than on the screen. When I was growing up, at one point, I didn't even like you—your characters. They treated the women so rotten, even though they were pretty and nice.

Gina Lollobrigida was *nice*?

Well, Doris Day was.

I know. I was a real asshole. *(Smiles.)*

You **said it. You know what it was? Your characters—in those comedies I grew up on—they never smiled, they were always so testy.**

It was part of my contract, Boze. Universal didn't allow me to smile, once I got on the set. I was a living doll before, and after . . . . Yeah . . . I was, uh, the straight man—the ladies got the laughs and the wardrobes, I got the billing and the big bucks. Fair tradeoff, right? I either huffed out the door or slung them over my shoulder at the end . . . I didn't feel very smiley, on a lot of sets.

And you were one of the first superstars—pardon my vulgarity here—in TV miniseries. Like "Wheels."

"Wheels" . . . a good experience. But you spend less time on a miniseries . . . A series can be murder, almost literally.

One of my editors called you "the worst interview in town."

That is true. Not my fault. I'd rather be worst interview than worst lay.

Can I just ask this: After being persuaded to wed, were you more resentful of what you had to do, privately, for your public image? Did you resent the press more after the divorce? You've done relatively little publicity ever since.

. . . She said some negative things. I reacted with pain and anger, then I became numb to the press. I stayed away, as much as I could. If I could, I went on TV, instead, when I had to publicize a picture. Then years passed, I didn't remarry, and they wondered. And *I* wouldn't feed them the same old fairy-tale pap they wanted to hear, and I wouldn't hurt my best interests, so they either ignored me or made up bland things.

They say—whoever *they* are—that bland publicity or no publicity can hurt a career more than bad publicity. Is that true?

Probably. I don't know.

You later had a bad experience with a *Look* journalist?

Some journalist! That was *during* the marriage; the writer was a bright girl, very charming. I was very taken with her. We had two or three interviews in New York and flew out together to Los Angeles. She came to the house and had dinner with us—Phyllis and I were still married. Very nice. Marvelous. Then out came this piece. The *first* sentence read: "Rock Hudson is a mechanical man; point him in the right direction, and he'll keep going until he bumps into something."

And it went on from there. It was a *slash,* and that was during the days when all that used to hurt. Now, screw it! I don't care what people write or think. But I'm not going to give them the chance to sink their fangs into me.

Yet in a way you've been lucky, Rock, because there's been very little innuendo; you don't often get asked about your sex life, do you?

Not as often as Liberace. In England, they ask, all right!

Phyllis was Henry Willson's secretary . . .

End of that subject—well, it's been nice knowing ya . . .

No, no: I'm not asking about her. Henry Willson also named Tab Hunter . . .

So do I and Tab have something in common? *(Smiles.)*

I know the answer to that one. Anyway, Willson also named Rhonda Fleming.

I get it: Did the man have *any* taste?

What was your relationship with him? Just an agent or . . . ?

How many people have walked out on you, Boze?

Just enough to make it interesting.

I think you figure it's integrity? Or what?

Would you like to do an autobiography?

If someone gave me a million dollars . . . Only in self-defense. Maybe to shock people with the truth. I'd wait till I'm old, though. Seventy's a good age for that kind of book. At seventy, it doesn't matter.

Tony Curtis told me he'd never do an autobiography, but he'd like to do a book about his father, about his own childhood. Would you enjoy writing or telling about growing up?

Let me think. . . . *(Smiles.)* Yeah. Sure. *Big Noise From Winnetka.* How's that for a title? Or is it too suggestive? *(Laughs.)* *Big Fart From Winnetka?*

God, Rock! And they think you're *bland*?

I'm not interested in any book. And I'm not interested *(warningly)* in having someone do my biography.

You know what someone *might* do? One of those filmographies—a films-of book. Would you mind that? And *I'm* not interested, just to ease your mind.

You're not? *(Mock-cries.)* Oh, gee. *(Smiles.)* Because I was *about* to say that would be awfully dull . . . You just did a book, didn't you?

So?

I want to look it up. See how nice you treated Jane. Fonda Jane, huh? *(Laughs.)* Were you *kind*? To tell the truth, I wouldn't mind. If *you* did it. I know I could trust you. *(Smiles gently.)*

Thanks . . . Rock, how many top actors in Hollywood do you think are gay?

Whew! Too many for me to name. If you mean gay, or

"bisexual"—whatever that really means—then maybe most. I guess if one came out, the crowding from the closet would be so strong, several would be *pushed* out. Trust me, Boze, America does not want to know.

Well, I wasn't planning on telling them. So don't worry your pretty little head.

(Smiles.) You mean I shouldn't worry my big pretty head?

What was James Dean like, and why didn't you two get along?

Just because you work with someone, doesn't mean you can tell or find out what makes them tick.

Is it true that on the set of *Darling Lili* Julie Andrews and her husband Blake Edwards teased you about being gay?

Some husband-and-wife teams can't call the kettle black . . . There's been too much written about that junky picture.

What is *Man's Favorite Sport*?

You tell me! *(Laughs.)*

You were sure a bastard to Paula Prentiss in that one, but I loved it. Come to think of it, in half your movies you were trying to avoid women . . .

Art imitates life. I think George Cukor said that. *(Smiles sarcastically.)*

Mr. Cukor is a delightful man.

I'd rather work with him than attend one of his parties.

But you've never worked with him.

Right . . . I was offered a part in that thing [*Sextette*] Mae West did, before she died. Cukor was gonna direct. He didn't—we both saw the writing on the wall. What a turkey!

Speaking of writing on the wall, I once saw some bathroom graffiti that said "Edith Head gives good wardrobe."

(Laughs.) I love it! Everybody says Edie's gay.

But there's no proof, is there?

Well, in most cases, there'll never be proof. Where's the proof that Tom Mix was straight?

Tom who? I'm just kidding; I've heard of him. So what didn't you like about George Cukor's parties? Or should that be singular?

It's okay, if you want to get out your party manners. "Mr. Ambassador, I should like to present one of our biggest stars, Mr. Rock Hudson." "*How* d'you do?" "How do *you* do?" "Fine, thank-yoh, and yoh?" And on and on and on. He gets all the ritziest people over to his house.

That is some house.

I could even envy him. (*Smiles.*) Except, I'd have the shrine to Saint Katharine [Hepburn] removed.

From several people, I've heard that she's anti-gay-males.

That's right: anti-gay-*males*.

Kenneth Anger says that's because her elder brother, who was supposedly gay, hung himself when he was sixteen or so.

And Katharine herself found the body. I've heard that. . . . Doesn't matter; I'll never work with her.

Do you regret not having worked with someone like Bette Davis?

Shit yes. Bette's a real fun broad, great sense of humor. I'd love to have seen her putting a director through his paces. She eats directors for breakfast.

What did you think when James Dean died only four days after completing *Giant*?

After completing *his* scenes . . . Tragic. Of course. And a big blow from out of the blue—one of those things no one expects. But I'll tell you what was more tragic, in a way, and that's when Monty [Clift] had that [car] accident that disfigured . . . that was the beginning of the end for him, a long drawn-out hell-on-earth time for the poor guy.

You were friends?

Friends . . . yeah. Listen, someday I'll make a list of "friends" and "more than friends," and everybody'll flip out. But not yet. But yeah, it was right after a party at Elizabeth's house—she was married to Michael Wilding. Monty left, and . . . well, everyone knows the rest. We all went down and found him . . . just . . . bleeding like you've never seen. It was terrible. *(Slowly inhales, then exhales.)*

Do you think if Monty had lived, he would eventually have come out?

(Nods.) I don't doubt it. He was pretty headstrong and icono-clastic.

Did you, or do you, think that coming out is simply self-destructive?

Not like taking drugs . . .

About "McMillan and Wife" . . .

That crappy thing?

Did you or didn't you get along with Susan Saint James?

We had our ups and downs . . . but I don't think anything would be served by either me or Susan being one-hundred-percent honest.

There's so much criticism of anyone in the public eye, with costars, critics, and others. How do you keep from becoming hard?

(Smiles suggestively.)

Too tough a cookie, maybe I should say.

(Chuckles.) Well, actors need a tough skin to take it. But on the other hand, you have to leave your mind open to be sensitive. Otherwise it's hard to do the job. A friend said something to me the other day. "No wonder actors tend to drink a lot." I never thought of it that way, but it's probably true.

You're quite a drinker yourself, Rock.

(Mock-haughtily.) Most legends are. But I've never had a drinking problem.

Meaning that getting a drink is never a problem?

(Both laugh.) . . . You just don't want to overdo.

What about smoking? You take the cake!

Yeah, I smoke. . . . *(Smiles.)* But everything goes full circle. As a child, you start out helpless, and as an old, feeble person, you end up helpless. You know, it's like acting: some actors start out in TV, then go on to being big movie stars. Then once the work starts getting less and further between, they return to television . . .

Would you be happy not working?

It's like what they say about women, because I can't live with it, and I can't live without it.

Are you still ambitious?

Shit no.

What about trying for another Oscar nomination?

You're dreaming, Boze. Either that, or you're pitching me some screenplay you just wrote.

No screenplay—honest. But you do like to work?

I'm a workaholic. I can't sit still.

Yet you're awfully picky.

I can afford to be.

I think part of it is, you're lazy. You'd rather sit by your pool with a tequila sunrise in one hand . . .

Preferably a martini.

With olive, of course.

Who's she? *(Both laugh.)* I love olives. *(Grins.)* I love the way that juicy little pimento strip gets shoved into that firm green olive . . .

You certainly have a novel way of looking at food.

Sure: man's two strongest urges.

Eating and boozing?

. . . (Smiles.)

Now, let's get back to the real Rock Hudson.

There is no real Rock Hudson. *(Winks.)* Hell, if you scratched and scratched beneath the surface of most of the roles I played, you wouldn't find any kind of human being there. *(Laughs dourly.)* I'm not like anyone I've ever played. Roy Fitzgerald is a different person from Rock Hudson, whom I sometimes think of as a stranger. The public doesn't know Roy, only Rock, who is partially of their own creation.

Of the heterosexual media's creation.

That suits me fine. . . . I've always been my *own* man.

Do you think you've ever lost a good role, or any role, because of your sexuality?

I *have.*

Not because a studio feared the public would find out?

No! That's all built-in—built-in protection. *You* know that no one's going to want to print the truth. That's not the problem.

What is?

Everyone knows about everybody in Hollywood—who sleeps with whom, who doesn't sleep, who does it standing on his head or in the dentist's chair. And some of those guys just don't like fairies.

You mean producers or directors or executives?

All of the above. They know there's thousands of homos on SAG's rolls [The Screen Actors Guild], and they'd rather hire the straights. *That's* the problem.

But how could one get around that?

You can't. It's not too hard to keep the public from knowing, but you'd have to be some kind of spy to keep the Industry from knowing. Fuck 'em.

You were the on-screen narrator of *Marilyn*, the documentary

that Fox compiled after her death. She was stigmatized, and limited, by the dumb-blonde label. Do you think there was something comparable for you?

(Nods head reluctantly.) Yessir. But it's worse, now. Hell, actors were *supposed* to be good-looking in the old days. Gable and Flynn and Ty Power—*Ty Power* . . . —and all the rest. That was all before Dustin Hoffman . . .

Here's something you probably don't know: Hoffman's first big break was as a crippled German homosexual in a play . . .

A crippled German homosexual?! *(Laughs.)* Not, you mean, a crippled homosexual German? Oh, I get it. Well, you're right—I didn't know; Roddy's the movie buff [Roddy McDowall], he knows all that kind of stuff. If they ever open a Hollywood museum, he'll be the curator.

So what do you think of the Hoffmans and De Niros, etc.?

They're good—damned good. But I always thought there was room for both of us.

Now good looks are out, right?

Not entirely. There's still Redford, a few other guys. But the best roles still go to the homely guys. In the old days, you looked like Ty Power, you went to Hollywood. Now, you go work in your local Chippendales [a Los Angeles male-strip nightclub].

You laugh a lot, Rock. What do you like to laugh at?

Sex. *(Smiles.)* To laugh at it and with it. Sex is really very funny, when you get down to it.

Rock, have you remained close with Jim Nabors? I know you don't see each other, even just as friends, in public . . .

We're still friends.

When you approach a new project, do you still get nervous?

I'll tell you what I do get: a good director. I can get very nervous without a good director. Shit, I probably wouldn't have gotten the Academy Award [nomination] without [George] Stevens's help.

Have you worked with many gay directors?

My share. *(Shrugs.)*

Fassbinder told me that he thinks gay directors have a better feel for relationships on screen. What do you think?

Probably. *(Shrugs.)*

I can see you're very passionate about moviemaking.

I *am*—next to television . . . I don't know *how* people can sit there, in front of it, for hours on end.

Depends what the alternative is, probably. One thing you enjoy doing in your spare time is boating, right?

Right.

That is to say, cruising . . . ?

That, too. On land and on sea. *(Smiles.)*

What kind of music do you especially like, Rock?

Rock music, of course! *(Laughs.)* And Mozart.

Mozart and a martini . . .

Mozart is better with burgundy.

Two burgundies, so it's stereo, right?

What's the difference? You lose count, anyway—and some of Mozart's pieces were pretty long.

Now, Mozart was apparently heterosexual.

One of the few composers who was.

You should have played a composer, along the way. Richard Chamberlain played Tchaikovsky, and . . .

Can you see me in a wig, Boze?

I hear you have one anyway.

What? . . . Oh! My Santa Claus wig—I keep that upstairs, for special occasions, like parties. I greet my guests with it on, sometimes.

Not a whole Santa outfit?

Shit no. From the neck down, you never know what I might have on, or off.

You're comfortable with nudity, aren't you?

If you've got it . . . *(Grins.)*

You're not the period picture kind, though. That's true.

People weren't as tall as me in those days.

They could always have Brooke Shields play your daughter.

And Redgrave could play my wife. Or sister.

They could call it *Revenge of the Six-Footers. (Both laugh.)* No, they couldn't. You're over six feet. I guess some parts are automatically closed to you, because of height.

I couldn't do a biography of Toulouse-Lautrec. I couldn't do *The Dustin Hoffman Story.*

Who would you want to play you if they made a movie—or a TV movie—of your life?

God forbid! But casting the right actor, physically, wouldn't be all that tough. . . . What a gruesome thought! *(Laughs.)*

You don't travel much.

You mean abroad?

Anywhere, apparently. Is it because you're too easily recognized?

Sometimes. Not with the Santa wig . . . *(Smiles.)* But I've been to, or near, the Shivwit Reservation. *(Smiles.)*

The *what*?

It's an Indian reservation near Saint George, Utah. Fantastic scenery.

Oh. Shivwit—the Shivwit Reservation; sounds more like a Jewish countryclub to me. *(Both laugh.)* How about overseas? Is there anyplace you haven't been that you'd love to go?

There's this holy mountain in Greece—they *call* it holy. I think it's called Mt. Athos. And it's only men—you can visit if you're a

man. They haven't allowed women in about a thousand years.
That ought to be interesting, huh? *(Winks.)*

But it's a monastery, probably.

So?

**So I imagine most of the time there is spent at services, or
making liqueur.**

See . . . ? *(Smiles.)*

**You're incorrigible. . . Were you at all offended when Doris
Day was nominated [for an Oscar] for *Pillow Talk*, but you
weren't? You did more acting than her, in that one.**

Not really. I mean, I wasn't upset, because in *Giant*, Elizabeth
wasn't nominated, and she was damned good. She'd never been
nominated. Of course, she soon took care of that! *(Laughs.)* [Taylor
later won two Oscars.] But believe it or not, *Pillow Talk* did win
something—some Best Screenplay award or other. Thelma Ritter
also got nominated [for Best Supporting Actress].

Oh, she was a doll, *the* character actress, I think.

(Nods.)

**I have a tiny bit of a quote from the *Time* review of *Send Me
No Flowers*, which was your last picture with Doris Day.**

What a sadist . . . *(Smiles.)*

**It says, "Actor Hudson, who is sensitively cast as a half-dead
hero, has seldom performed so inoffensively. And Actress Day,
40, should maybe stop trying to play Goldilocks." How do you
feel about that today?**

I never heard that.

Come on! *Time*? You never read reviews?

I get them read to me. But that one was funny. I love how they
said I performed inoffensively. That's always a compliment, isn't
it? Poor Doris—in those days, 40 was a dirty word. At least they
didn't mention my age—I wasn't much younger.

**Did you stop making movies together because of reviews like
this?**

I think the wave had peaked. I had more interesting offers. *(Shrugs.)*

There's also talk of a *Pillow Talk* sequel, just as there's been talk of a *Giant* sequel . . .

(Makes yakkety-yak gestures with hand.)

True . . . You played with Lollobrigida twice . . .

(Mock look of horror, then laughs.)

. . . and Claudia Cardinale twice. But not even once with Sophia Loren, one of my favorites. How come?

(Shrugs.) Tab Hunter, as you say, *played* with her, so . . . *(Shrugs.)* Interchangeable.

You and Tab are interchangeable?

On *screen.*

Would you say you've ever given a performance that was underrated?

. . . Mmm-hmm. *Seconds.*

I don't recall that one.

No one's seen it. John Frankenheimer directed. Drama. Now it's kind of a cult film—that no one's seen. Maybe they'll rediscover it someday.

You were rather instrumental in helping Lee Majors become an actor . . .

(Guffaws.)

Didn't you . . . ?

That's that; next question.

I saw a picture of you once, on the diving board of the Beverly Hills Hotel.

Salad days. Fifties or sixties?

I don't know. You looked the same—until the mustache.

One of those big, boxy pairs of trunks, right?

Right. Did you do a lot of beefcake in the early days?

The early days and the middle days. *(Grins.)*

There's another memorable photo, but it's of you and several Paramount superstars, standing on steps. You and Lee Marvin, John Wayne, Barbra Streisand . . . I'm not sure who else.

Eastwood, Yves Montand—I think that's it, other than Bob Evans, our shepherd. *(Smiles.)* That was back in '68, '69, when we were all making big-budget duds. I was in *Darling Lili*, and Miss Andrews—God bless her—was supposed to be in the photo with us. We all waited and waited. . . . Finally, Duke made some semi-obscene remark about our fair lady, and he got the photographer to go ahead and take the picture. Streisand was getting antsy, too—but it turned out to her benefit; she was the only female in the picture. *(Smiles.)*

So Barbra was on time and Julie wasn't. One usually reads it the other way around.

That's the fuckin' image thing. . . . Barbra was okay. Funny, making remarks—she kept saying how time was money and how much this picture—the photo—was costing the Paramount brass.

Who do you miss, of the people in Hollywood who have passed away?

(Smiles sadly.) Errol Flynn. He was a great guy. Everybody liked him.

You were close friends?

For a while.

What do you think of biographies that posthumously reveal an actor's sex life?

You mean his *gay* sex life? If you're a child-molester, as long as you're straight, it gets covered while you're still here to make jokes about it. Or to flee the country [as Roman Polanski did].

Well, it's come out about Power and Flynn, and Elsa Lanchester

did that introduction to the Charles Laughton book, saying that her late husband was gay . . . What do you think?

Why not? *(Shrugs.)* But most people never read that, or they don't believe it.

You don't disapprove because it might "tarnish" someone's reputation?

Come on, now—only with bigots, and so long as the bigots aren't your bosses . . . By then, it doesn't make a hell of a lot of difference. I just think people eventually get tired of the lies. Even the public would rather know the truth.

You think so?

Well, whether they want to know it or not, they have to get to accept people for what they are.

Do you think the average gay man or woman should come out of the closet?

(Shrugs.) It's up to him, or it's up to her. Depends what they have to lose.

Rock, do you think you were born gay?

Probably. *(Smiles.)* But only after I came out of the womb.

There is a scene in the second Rock Hudson/Doris Day opus, *Lover Come Back*, in which Rock dons Doris's nightgown, the only apparel handy. Out in public, a male onlooker tells his buddy, "He's the last guy I would've suspected . . ."
If Rock Hudson had died of cancer or a heart attack, his death would likely have received small press attention. But once it became known that he had AIDS, everyone took a second, long look at him. Despite his own reticence and that of his mostly gay associates, Rock's homosexuality finally became a worldwide secret. Not long before AIDS struck, Rock was offered the butch-gay role in Allan Carr's *La Cage Aux Folles*. The part had been performed by Gene Barry, then Van Johnson, and Rock enjoyed the musical enormously. But he declined. Immediately after Rock's death, a longtime associate went on television to deny that he was "necessarily" gay. Ditto a few misguided print and TV columnists.

One tabloid even reprinted Rock's own words—from the closeted interviews—as proof of so-called normalcy.

The media overkill betrayed homophobia at all levels, from the respected newsweeklies down to the gutter press. But it also made the public more aware of AIDS, showed that it could afflict the rich, famous, and admired, and it indirectly helped boost funding for AIDS research and care of AIDS victims. Besides which, Rock's coming out—voluntarily or not—was proof that not all, and not even most, gay men fit into the stereotype which Hollywood fashioned and perpetuated. Rock Hudson was famous long before there was AIDS. He will be famous long after AIDS.

Epilogue

I THINK it was Noel Coward who said that most conversations are basically competing monologues. He meant, of course, between peers. Between mere mortal and celebrity—that is, somebody written about after the inconvenience of death—words are less taken for granted. At least by the interviewer, who unlike a casual converser is more apt to actively listen and retain.

Yet such sessions may yield some frustration, for one seldom glimpses more than an aspect, or *rôle*, of a given celebrity. And most interviewees are selective, sometimes lazy, about what they share. Months before interviewing Fassbinder, I had a book published on Jane Fonda's films. Unbeknownst to me, Fassbinder had sought to make *Rosa L.*, later described as "Europe's *Reds*." The bio-pic of activist Rosa Luxemburg was to have starred Fonda, who'd favorably discussed the project with Fassbinder.

But when I mentioned the actress and my book, the writer-director seemed bored. Or sleepy. I also brought up Rock Hudson, and much later read Fassbinder's description of Hudson's character in Douglas Sirk's *Written on the Wind* as "the most pig-headed bastard in the world" for not acknowledging Dorothy Malone's pining character. Fassbinder briefly noted his admiration for Sirk to me. The German-American had directed Hudson in eight movies, yet neither subject was one which Fassbinder strove—if such an energetic verb could apply—to pursue.

On the sunnier side of ego, George Cukor never alluded to his long-standing charitable efforts vis-à-vis Hollywood's once-glittering dispossessed. And Rock Hudson, unlike many megastars, never declaimed about having been one of Hollywood's five biggest box-office draws for eight years in a row, from 1957 to 1964. Hudson no more than touched on Cukor. Cukor likewise didn't spotlight Hudson. Their reticence came, I think, from a sense of brother-hood, not the typical stellar aversion to acknowledgment of Sig-nificant Others.

Like most actors inside or outside the profession, the former "Baron of Beefcake" was a complex individual. During his lifetime, I heard various stories purportedly illustrating Hudson's modesty, aloofness, joie de vivre, or self-destructiveness. After his death came the public tributes, some well-intended, some meant to di-vorce the man from his natural sexuality.

One story will suffice. In the early fifties Rock was in England making *The Sea Devils*. His friend actor-director Bryan Forbes in-vited him to afternoon tea. The smallish meal used up the Forbes household's butter ration for the month. After Rock found out, he sent food parcels until Forbes begged him to stop.

My friend Enrico Zanghi sent me a quote attributed to Hudson after his open-heart surgery—"How blue is the day to the eye that's been blinded." I still remember Rock with a grin on his handsome face, or laughing heartily. The sound of man's laughter reverberates through my memories of these subjects, save the chemically distorted Fassbinder.

But in between the laughter and the stories told and untold, I discerned the advice and experience of my surrogate uncles. Today I see this verbal odyssey for what it was: a journey within and beyond myself; a series of conversations with men who, as I grow older, become younger and younger to me.